PAPUA NEW GUINEA

Social Science

Grade 8

Stephen Ranck

OXFORD

Level 8, 737 Bourke Street, Docklands, Victoria 3008, Australia

Oxford University Press is a department of the University of Oxford. It furthers the University's objective of excellence in research, scholarship, and education by publishing worldwide in

Oxford New York

Auckland Cape Town Dar es Salaam Hong Kong Karachi Kuala Lumpur Madrid Melbourne Mexico City Nairobi New Delhi Shanghai Taipei Toronto

With offices in

Argentina Austria Brazil Chile Czech Republic France Greece Guatemala Hungary Italy Japan Poland Portugal Singapore South Korea Switzerland Thailand Turkey Ukraine Vietnam

OXFORD is a trademark of Oxford University Press in the UK and in certain other countries

First published 2007
Reprinted 2008, 2009 (twice), 2010 (twice), 2014 (twice), 2015, 2017, 2018, 2020, 2022, 2024

ISBN 978 0 19 555512 7

Typeset by Palmer Higgs Pty Ltd
Illustrated by Uramina and Nelson Pty Lty and diacriTech
Maps by MAPgraphics Pty Ltd
Printed in Singapore by Markono Print Media Pte Ltd

Contents

Introduction

WHAT ARE WE GOING TO DO WITH SOCIAL SCIENCE IN GRADE 8?

In this book we are going to explore the whole world, as well as Papua New Guinea.

You will be able to look at many other countries in this course. You already have many tools for your study. In Years Six and Seven, you have looked at local, national and regional areas. Remember how careful you must be in the social sciences with values and attitudes. The same principles apply when you look at the whole world.

Studying the world will build on everything you did before. We looked at your local area, Papua New Guinea and the regions around us. All that is part of the world but now we add many more countries to our studies. This year is only a start. You can spend all your life learning more about the world and the basic concepts covered in this book will help you do this.

The physical earth

The land, water and atmosphere are interconnected around our **globe**. We will look at some of the world's main physical features. Then we look at how people have settled around the world. We will see how people adapt and use the world's resources. Finally we will look at world hazards and what we can do about them.

Different types of government

We will look at governments and societies from history, and how people have become more connected. We will look at world trade in past and present times. We will look at how countries have tried to work together and the problems they have had. We will also look at a case study on slavery. This is an area where the world has made great progress in human rights.

Culture around the world

We will look at cultures in many ways, including different world cultures and growing global culture. This is the culture that everyone on Earth shares. We will look at the good and the bad in culture. We will look at what we share and do not share in culture. And we will look at ways of protecting world culture.

An integrating project

You can select any of the materials covered in the first three chapters. You may do a study on another nation of the world. You may do a study on an international organisation. You can compare what is happening in Papua New Guinea with another nation or other parts of the world. There are plenty of examples to learn from. You have almost **infinite** choices. You can start a list now of places you do not know about or want to learn about.

Review

Now is a good time to review some of the concepts covered in Years Six and Seven. What can you remember? Look at each concept in the table. How are these concepts used in social science studies? How can you use them in studying the world?

Values	Bias	Rights	Good behaviour	Social science process
Attitudes	Roles	Sustainability	Bad behaviour	Failure to adapt
Prejudice	Responsibilities	Behaviour	Adaptation	Other concepts

Look at the world maps on the front and back covers. How do you think these concepts will apply to different places in the world?

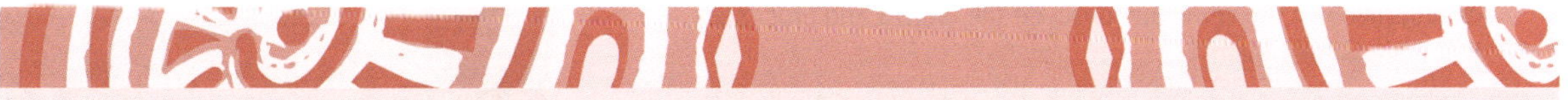

Throughout this book you will see key words in **bold** type. You can find these words and their definitions in the glossary at the back of this book.

1 People and the Environment

Chapter summary

In this chapter you will have the opportunity to:

✓ look at the physical and natural environments of the world

✓ look at some of the major features of human settlement around the world

✓ look at how some resources are used around the world

✓ investigate some major global hazards and human responses to these hazards.

Syllabus references

Syllabus strand: Environment and Resources

Syllabus sub-strand: People and environment

Outcomes

8.1.1: Students are able to compare and contrast the main physical environments of the world and describe the factors and processes that have formed them.

8.1.2: Students are able to analyse how physical environments influence human settlement patterns in the world.

8.1.3: Students are able to evaluate the impact of resource use on the world's physical environments and human settlement patterns.

8.1.4: Students are able to identify international examples of sustainable practices to the natural environment and propose possible solutions to problems.

8.1.5: Students are able to identify and describe the causes and effects of hazardous natural events in other parts of the world and how people respond to them.

Papua New Guinea and the world

THE PHYSICAL WORLD

The physical world is where we all live. The physical **environment** provides us with much of what we need to live. Scientists study the physical world. Social scientists study the people of the world. They study how people interact with each other and how they interact with the physical world. Social and physical scientists study the past and present. Then they can make **predictions** about the future.

Our home is a planet. Here is a view of planet Earth from outer space.

For you to try

Look at the map on the inside front cover.

- What are the two main features on this map? What other features can you find? What do you think are the most important features?
- What features on the map do we need to stay alive? What features are missing that we need to stay alive?

Planet Earth

Scientists think that the Earth is about four and a half billion years old. (That is 4 500 000 000 years old). They also think that our **universe** is about 13 billion years old. No one knows what happened before that or what will happen to the universe in the future. Science can help us find answers about what is happening on Earth, and what will happen on Earth in the future.

The planet Earth is a **sphere**. It is round like an orange or a soccer ball but much bigger! A planet is a large body of material that **orbits** the sun. Scientists now agree that there are eight planets. There are also many other objects that orbit the sun.

Our planet is about 150 million kilometres away from the sun. The Earth sits at a slight angle to the sun, creating different seasons in different parts of the world. The Earth **rotates** on its axis every 24 hours as it travels around the sun. This gives us day and night. The Earth's rotation makes it look like the sun goes around the Earth, rising in the east and setting in the west. That is an illusion. When you see the sun coming up, it is really the Earth turning you closer to the sun as it rotates towards the east.

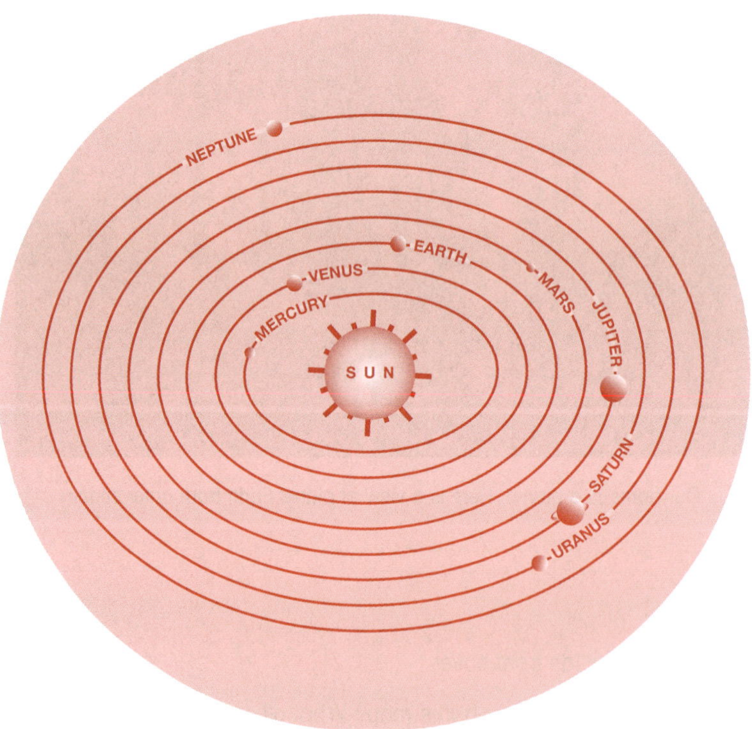

Earth takes 365¼ days, or one year, to orbit the sun.

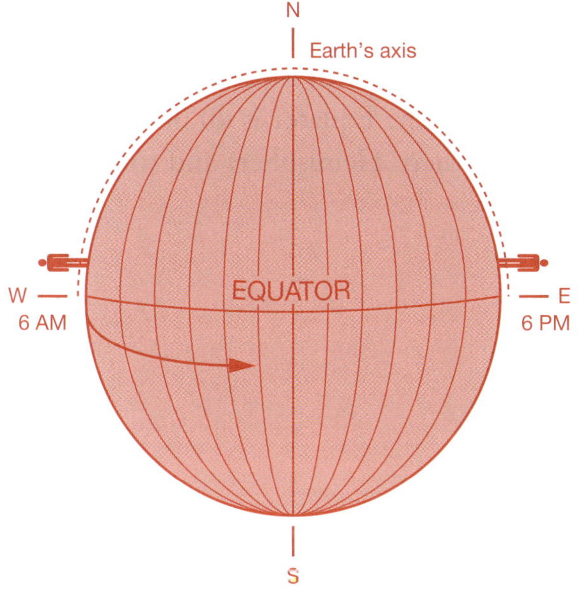

In this diagram, the Earth is turning on its axis. A student is standing on each side of the Earth. It is 6 a.m. for one student and 6 p.m. for the other. If we had a total of 24 students spread evenly around the Earth, there would be an hour's time difference between each student. These time differences are called 'time zones'.

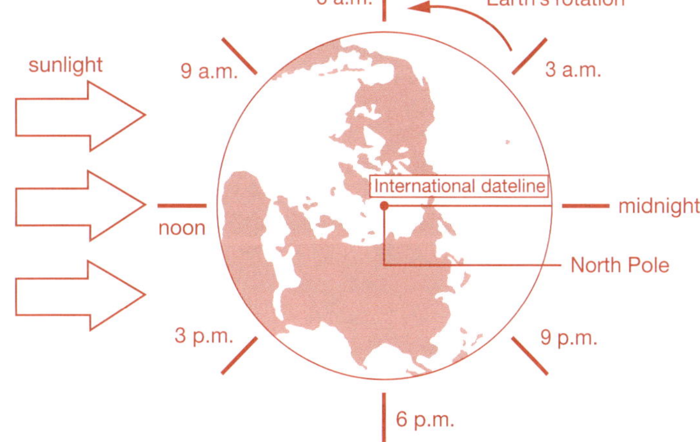

This diagram shows a view of the Earth from above the North Pole. It is turning on its axis. The new day starts at an imaginary line in the Pacific Ocean called the 'International Dateline'.

For you to try

- What islands see the new day first? What islands are the last ones to see the new day?
- Where can you travel so you leave on Monday and arrive on Sunday? Is this travelling backwards in time?
- How many time zones does Papua New Guinea have? And Australia?

Earth is just the right distance from the sun to support life. It is not too hot and not too cold. If it were closer to the sun, the heat could boil away the atmosphere and water, like on the planet Mercury. Or we might have a very hot and poisonous atmosphere, like the planet Venus. Planets that are too far from the sun are too cold. Earth provides just the right physical environment to support life.

Mapping the world

We have many ways to describe a specific location on Earth. Earth is divided into two **hemispheres**. There is one on each side of the **Equator**. The Equator is 40 000 km long. It goes right around the Earth. To the north is the Northern Hemisphere and to the south is the Southern Hemisphere.

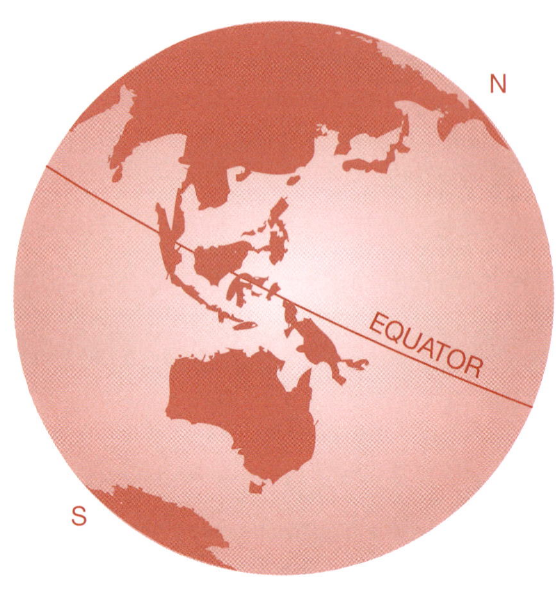

For you to try

- Use a map to find the hemisphere in which the following countries are located:

Colombia	England
New Zealand	Uganda
Ecuador	Indonesia
Papua New Guinea	United States of America

- Use a map to find the hemisphere in which the following continents are located:

North America	South America
Australia	Europe
Africa	Asia

- What differences do you think you would find living in the Northern Hemisphere?

We can use a **grid** to locate any place on the Earth's surface. When we put a grid on a sphere, we have two different sets of lines. These are called the lines of **longitude** and the lines of **latitude**. Lines of latitude run parallel to each other. They show locations north and south of the Equator. Lines of longitude run around the Earth. They show locations east and west of the **Prime Meridian**. The Prime Meridian is found in Greenwich, in England.

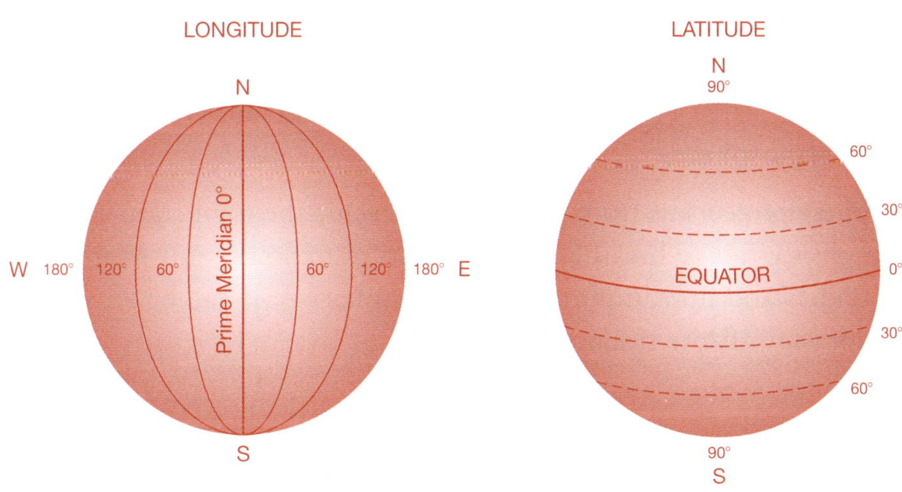

We can measure location in degrees. There are 360 degrees in a circle. There is only a quarter of a circle from the Equator to North Pole and from the Equator to the South Pole. So there are 90 degrees of latitude north of the Equator, and 90 degrees of latitude south of the Equator. There is half a circle on each side of the Prime Meridian. So there are 180 degrees of longitude to the east of the Prime Meridian, and 180 degrees of longitude to the west of the Prime Meridian.

To describe location, we give the longitude in degrees east or west of the Prime Meridian first. Then we give the latitude in degrees north or south of the Equator. For example, Central Africa is 20 degrees east of the Prime Meridian and 10 to 20 degrees south of the Equator. Each degree can be divided into 60 minutes. Each minute can be divided into 60 seconds. We can use minutes and seconds to describe locations in even more detail.

For you to try

- Use a map to find the longitude and latitude of the following locations:
  North Island of New Zealand	Cuba	The centre of Madagascar
  The centre of the Pyrenees	Central Japan
- Remember to find the longitude first, then the latitude – you can remember this by remembering the statement 'First walk to the coconut, then climb the tree'.

The Earth's surface

Two main features on the Earth's surface are water and land. Water can be divided into fresh water and the oceans. The land is made up of continents. There is another major feature. It is the **atmosphere**.

The atmosphere protects us from the sun. It prevents the temperature from getting too hot or cold. It gives us air to breathe. And it affects our climate and weather. People are beginning to understand how important the atmosphere is. It can be affected by human activity. It is a precious **finite** resource.

Climate zones

The atmosphere interacts with water and land, causing winds. Winds are very important in making climate zones. There is a worldwide system of winds. This system carries warm and cold air long distances around the world. It can carry warm air away from warm areas. It can carry cold air away from cold areas. We call this worldwide wind system the general **circulation** of the atmosphere. The land, the water and the Earth's rotation around the sun also affect climate zones.

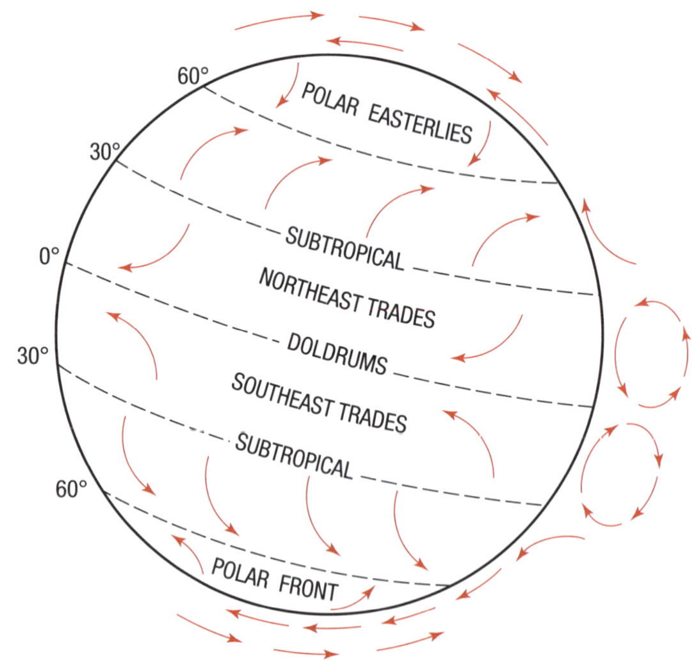

he **subtropical** zone is often dry. Temperatures an vary, especially in the desert. The clear skies let eat escape at night. So temperatures can be cold t night and over 40°C during the day. Trade winds low between the subtropical and tropical zones. his creates areas that are drier than the tropics, but vetter than subtropical deserts. These areas have wo seasons. One is wet and one is dry. There s enough rain to support grasslands. his is lush and green in the vet season. But it is ry and brown and rone to bushfires n the dry eason.

The **tropical** zone is wet and warm. It starts at the Equator.

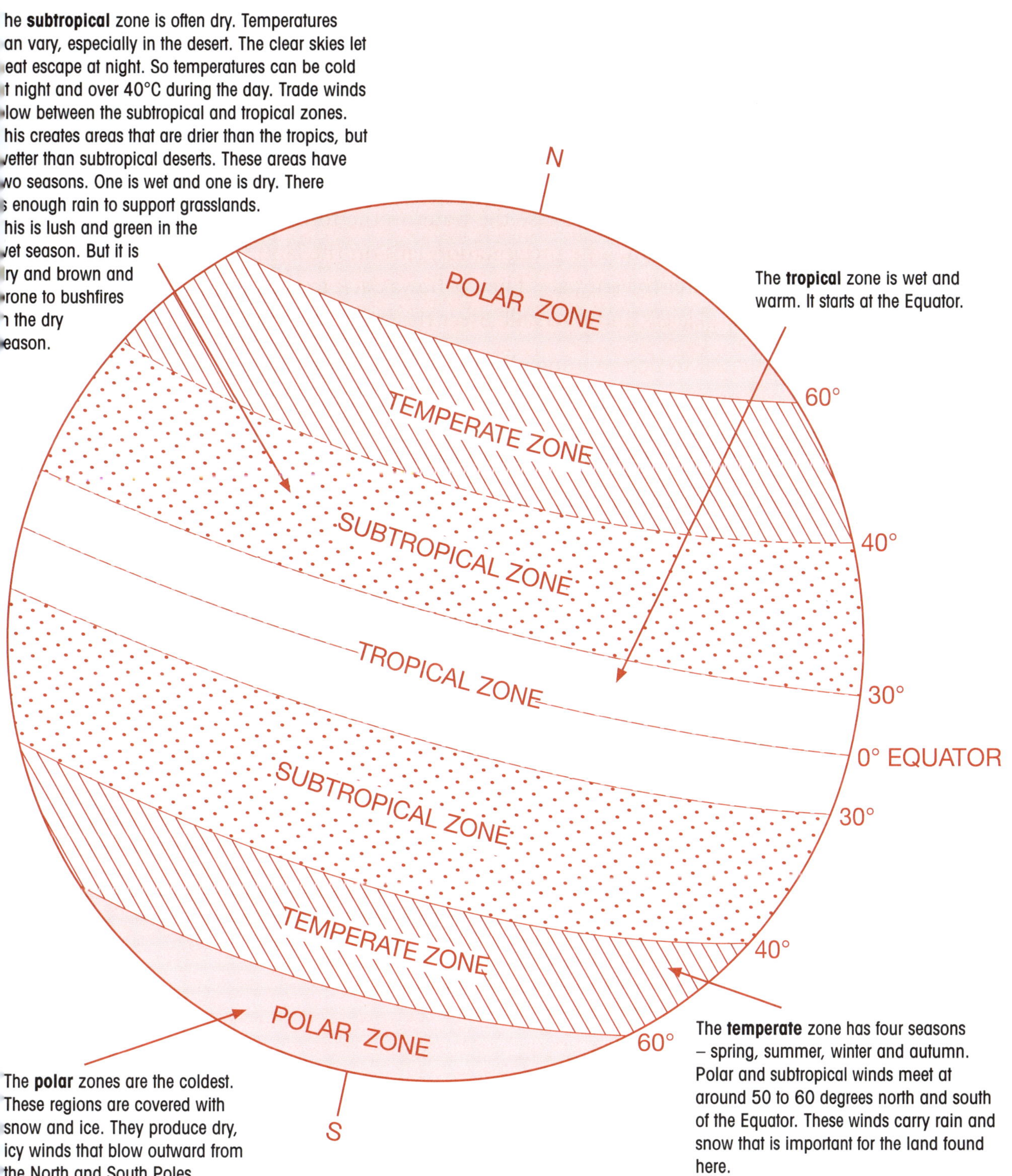

The **polar** zones are the coldest. These regions are covered with snow and ice. They produce dry, icy winds that blow outward from the North and South Poles.

The **temperate** zone has four seasons – spring, summer, winter and autumn. Polar and subtropical winds meet at around 50 to 60 degrees north and south of the Equator. These winds carry rain and snow that is important for the land found here.

Oceans

Oceans cover nearly three quarters of the Earth's surface. No other planet in our solar system has as much water as Earth. Like the atmosphere, the oceans are made up of different layers. These layers have different pressures and temperatures.

The oceans are the starting point of the water cycle. The sun heats and **evaporates** the water. This forms clouds. The clouds release the water in the form of rain, sleet, hail or snow. This is called **precipitation**. The precipitation falls on the land. It nourishes the vegetation and provides water for animals. Then it flows back to the ocean in rivers and glaciers. Rain and snow, glaciers and rivers all affect the land.

The oceans are essential to determining climates. They act like a bank. They collect and store heat instead of money. They distribute this heat through **currents**. Some of the biggest ocean currents carry heat for great distances. The Gulf Stream is a huge warm current in the Atlantic Ocean. It carries over a hundred times more water than all the rivers on Earth. The Gulf Stream carries warm water from the Gulf of Mexico north along the east coast of North America to the mid-Atlantic Ocean. It provides warm wind and rain that reaches Europe. If the Gulf Stream stopped, much of Europe would be covered in snow and ice. It would have a very different physical environment.

The water cycle carries water from the sea to the land and back to the sea.

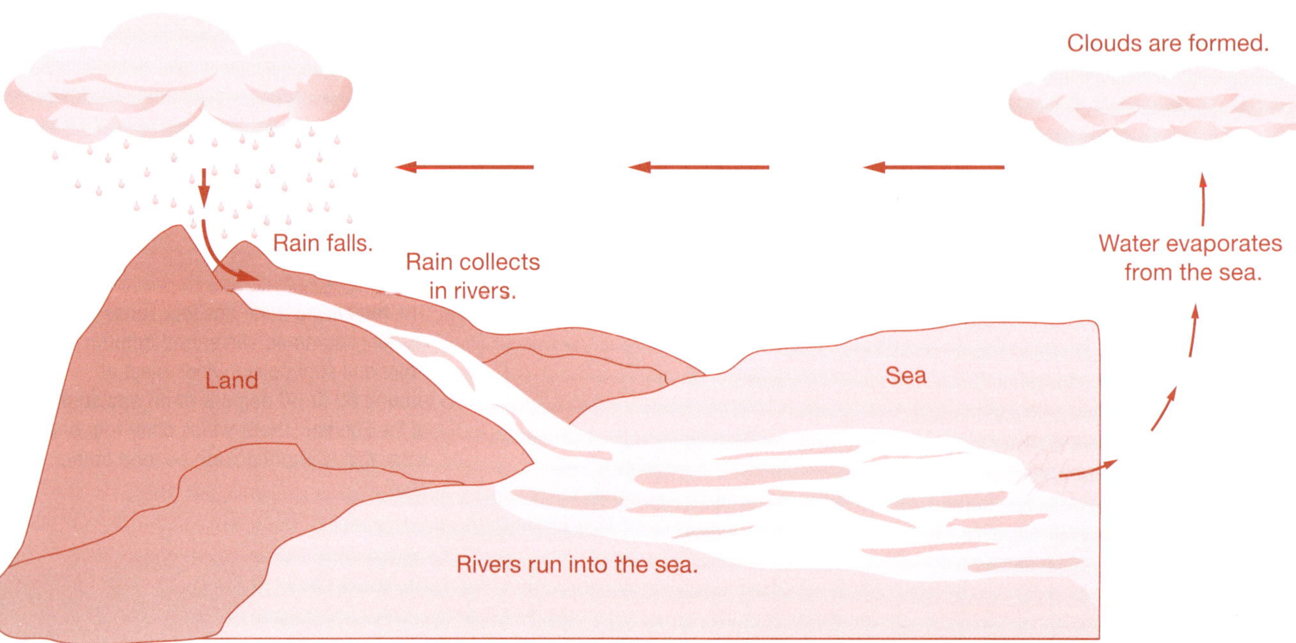

For you to try

- Use a map to locate the major oceans – the Pacific, the Atlantic, the Indian and the Arctic Oceans. Find the places where these oceans meet. What other saltwater seas or lakes can you find on the map?

Continents

The continents are the major landmasses on Earth. There are seven continents – Africa, Antarctica, Asia, Australia, Europe, North America and South America. Some continents are joined together. Australia is surrounded by water. It is called an 'island continent'. Some people believe that North America and South America are all part of one continent connected by Central America. They call this continent America.

In Year Seven, you studied **continental drift** and how continents were formed. Continents move slowly on **tectonic plates**. This movement has created mountain ranges and other physical features on the Earth's surface over millions of years. New Guinea is situated on the same tectonic plate as Australia. This plate is called 'Sahul'.

The coasts of South America and Africa are separated by the Atlantic Ocean. Look at the map on the inside front cover. You can see how the two coasts may have fitted together and moved apart over millions of years. This is a good example of continental drift.

Parts of some continents are underwater. Where the continent meets the sea is called the **continental shelf**. This is an area of relatively shallow water. It may have islands that are actually part of the continent. It can also be a valuable area for fisheries.

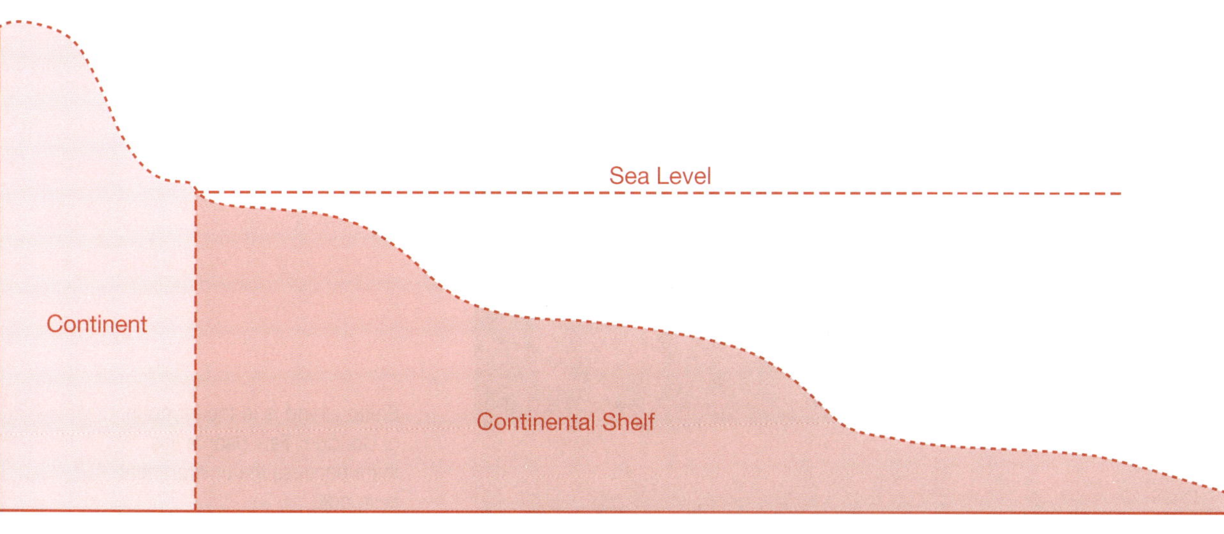

Antarctica is one of the least explored continents. It is covered with ice but receives very little precipitation. It has the highest average elevation of any of the continents.

For you to try

Locate the seven continents on a map.

- Which continents are joined together? Which continents are surrounded by water? Which continent has no real permanent settlement?
- Which continents have the most countries? Which continents have the least countries?
- Does it matter if people learn there are six or seven continents? Does it make a difference to their culture? Does it make a difference to their history? Does it make a difference to their worldview? Does it make a difference to their values and attitudes?

Islands

Islands are smaller landmasses than continents. Some, like the Hawaiian Islands, are created by volcanoes. Others, like Fiji, have separated from a continent and become surrounded by ocean. And others are created by the build-up of mud or sand over time. **Atolls**, like Kiribati, are coral islands. Can you think of any other way an island might be formed?

Baffin Island is in the far north of Canada. Few people live there because the environment is so cold.

The ten largest islands in the world	
Island	**Area in square kilometres**
Greenland	2 175 600 sq km
New Guinea	792 500 sq km
Borneo	725 500 sq km
Madagascar	587 000 sq km
Baffin	507 500 sq km
Sumatra	427 300 sq km
Honshu	227 400 sq km
Great Britain	218 100 sq km
Victoria	217 300 sq km
Ellesmere	196 200 sq km

For you to try

- In what different ways can you group the ten islands? Which ones do you know about?
- Divide the class into three groups. Each group can study three of the islands from the list. Compare them to New Guinea.
- The largest island in the world is called Greenland. Most of it is covered in ice and snow. So why do you think it was called Greenland? (Hint: could this be early advertising for settlers?)

Mountains

Mountains are found where the land rises up steeply to over 300 metres. Many mountains are grouped together. They are connected in chains or ranges. The Owen Stanley is a good example of a mountain range in Papua New Guinea. All the continents have some major mountain ranges. Some of the ranges form larger groups or belts of mountains.

Different forces create the mountain ranges. Tectonic plates coming together can push land upwards. This can also create weak spots where **magma** is released. This forms volcanoes. The Andes in South America include a number of volcanoes.

Important mountain ranges	
Name	**Location**
The American Cordillera	A 'cordillera' is a chain of mountains. The American Cordillera are the mountains that look like the backbone of the American continents. They start in Alaska and run south to the bottom of South America.
The Himalayas	This is the largest mountain group in the world and contains the world's highest peaks. They are found in Asia, running through the north of India, parts of Pakistan and China, all of Tibet, Nepal and Bhutan.
The Alps	This is a major mountain group in Europe. They start in France, covering Switzerland, parts of Italy, Austria, Slovenia and Croatia.

For you to try

Locate the mountain ranges in the table on a map. Find the length and width of each group. Try to measure it on your map or in an atlas.

- What cities are located in these mountains? Who are the people who live in these mountains? Can you find any information about places, people or resources in these mountains?
- Can you find any other mountain ranges on your map?
- Can you find examples of mountain ranges that create the border between countries? Why do you think this occurs?

Snow falls on high mountains. When it melts, water runs down into rivers, lakes and the sea.

Can you guess why we don't say the Alps mountains, the Himalayas mountains or the Andes mountains? It is because each one of these words means 'mountains' in the local language. If you say 'Andes Mountains', you are really saying 'mountains mountains'. That doesn't make sense! In fact, the word 'alp' actually means 'tall mountain'.

Rivers

Rivers are a major natural feature of the world. Rivers coming down from steep mountains flow very quickly. Others travel much more slowly over flatter areas. Rivers are parts of drainage systems. They let extra water flow from the land out to the sea or into a lake. Rivers help to create many special environments around the world.

For you to try

- Use a map to find some of the world's great rivers. Can you find the Blue and the White Nile? Can you find the Orinoco River? What other information can you find about the rivers in the table on the following page?

The Murray River is part of the largest river system in Australia. Compare what you see in this picture with some of the rivers you know about in Papua New Guinea.

The longest rivers on the continents		
River	**Continent**	**Length in kilometres**
The Nile – the longest river in the world	Africa	6 600 km
The Amazon – the second longest river in the world	South America	6 300 km
Chang Jiang – also called the Yangtze River	Asia	5 800 km
Huang He – also called the Yellow River	Asia	4 700 km
The Mackenzie River	North America	4 200 km
The Mississippi River – forms a very big river system when combined with the Missouri River	North America	3 800 km
The Murray-Darling River system	Australia	3 700 km

Grasslands

About a quarter of all the land on Earth is covered with grasses. Six continents have grasslands. These are usually flat areas covered with grasses, flowers and herbs. There are temperate and tropical grasslands. A steppe is an area where the land has been lifted upwards. The result looks like grassed terraces or steps.

Horses have long been used for work and transport on grasslands in Asia, Europe, North and South America.

Climate and soil determine which places have grasslands. The average yearly rainfall has to be sufficient to grow grass. Sometimes there is enough rain to sustain a few trees on the grassland. This area is called a savannah. Rain may only come at certain times of the year so droughts can also be common in grassland and savannah areas. A result of this is frequent fires that may destroy young trees but maintain the grass. The roots of the grass can survive fires and quickly send up shoots with the first rain. The soils of most grassland areas tend to be thin. They often have little nutrients, making it hard to grow trees and other large plants.

Some of the most famous grasslands are the savannahs of Africa. They support many herds of large grass-eating animals. These animals support the meat-eating animals. One lion can be supported for every 100 zebras or antelopes.

Forests

An evergreen pine forest.

Forests are made up of trees. The three main types of forest are tropical, temperate and evergreen. The largest forests are found in the Northern Hemisphere. They stretch across Canada and Siberia. They are evergreen forests made up of pine and spruce trees. They can survive in very cold temperatures. Similar types of trees exist in the Southern Hemisphere, but there is less land area and therefore less forest. The other **evergreen** forests are tropical rainforests found in South America, Africa, Asia and Australasia. **Deciduous** forests are found in the temperate climate zones. Trees in these forests lose their leaves each year in autumn. New leaves start to grow in spring. The forests are green and lush in summer.

Deforestation in South America.

The Food and Agriculture Organisation is part of the United Nations. In 2007, it found that forests covered nearly four billion hectares or almost one third of the world's land area. It also found that the world is losing forests. Ten countries have two thirds of all the world's forest areas: Australia, Brazil, Canada, China, the Democratic Republic of the Congo, India, Indonesia, Peru, the Russian Federation and the United States of America. Millions of hectares of forests are destroyed each year. South America has been losing around 4.3 million hectares per year between 2000 and 2005.

For you to try

- Use a map to find the countries with the most forest. What type of forests do you think are located in each country? Discuss your reasons in class.
- Why are forests important? How many uses can think of for them?

Deserts

Very dry places are called deserts. About one fifth of the world's land is covered by desert. Some deserts are made of sand dunes. But sandy deserts are only a small part of deserts around the world. Most deserts have plant life. Many deserts are rocky or covered with stone.

The word 'gobi' means 'place of stones'. The Gobi desert of central Asia is a stony place.

The plants and animals of deserts have adapted to conserve moisture. Many of the plants are covered with thorns or spines. This is to protect them from animals that want to eat them. Many desert animals only come out at night in places where the deserts are hot and dry. Rainfall is less than 15 centimetres a year on average. In cold deserts, it may snow instead of rain.

Some of the driest deserts are found in central Asia, Africa and the Pacific coast of South America. The Tibetan Plateau has the highest deserts in the world. Antarctica is sometimes called the coldest desert, but most people do not classify it as a desert. The Atacama desert is the driest desert on Earth. It is located on the south coast of Peru and the north coast of Chile. It can go ten years without rain.

Human activity is creating more deserts. This is called 'desertification'. The Sahara desert in Africa is growing larger. A big problem occurs when herders have too many animals eating the plants on grazing land. The plants cannot reproduce and the land turns to desert.

In Inner Mongolia, people have too many sheep and goats. The land cannot support so many animals so desertification is happening. Sand dunes are taking over these fields.

For you to try

- Use a map to find the largest desert areas in the world. What are the nearest deserts to Papua New Guinea?

Biosphere

The biosphere is the part of the Earth that supports life. We have already looked at the three main parts of the biosphere. They are the land, the water and the atmosphere. We can see that the three parts are linked. A change to any one part will affect the other two parts. For example, where water gets warmer, this will affect the atmosphere above. It will change the weather or climate. Those changes will then affect the land. We can also see that human activity affects the biosphere.

Settling the world

Homo sapiens is the name scientists give to modern humans. That is all of us. The remains of the first modern humans come from Africa. They are about 200 000 years old. They were found in Omo Kibish, in Ethiopia. These people spread west, south and to the northeast.

Groups of modern humans began to leave Africa around 70 000 years ago. World climates were colder. It was the last ice age. Sea levels were lower than they are today. This might have made it easier to travel. Or people may have been making better canoes and boats to travel along the coasts.

No one is sure how long it took to populate the world with modern humans. We do know that all of us are related to the people who left Africa 70 to 50 000 years ago. We don't know how many different groups left, why they travelled or how they travelled. All we have today is the evidence of arrivals from a few places around the world.

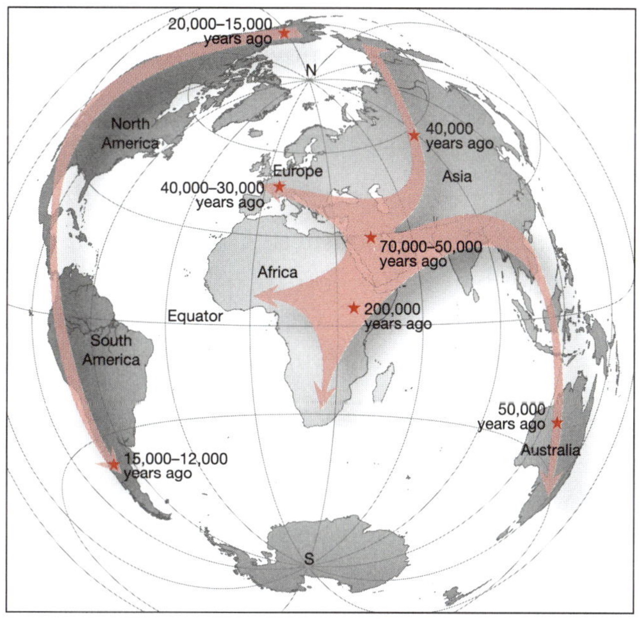

This map shows clues about human migration for the last 200 000 years. The clues give us some idea about what has happened. There is much we do not know. We learn more every time a scientist finds a new clue.

For you to try

Find Ethiopia on the map of human migration.

Look at the age of the different places. Each time a new place is found, this type of map changes.

- What do you think the different dates tell us? Is there enough information?
- How important is it to know what early people did?
- Where do you think they travelled the fastest? Where was travel slow?

People left Africa to come to Asia and Australia first. Then they started settling in Europe. Early Asians started moving into the Americas perhaps 20 000 years ago. And there is still no real permanent settlement in Antarctica. There are only scientific bases. (One baby was born at the Argentinean base. Argentina claimed this showed permanent settlement, but that baby is not there any more!)

Growing numbers of people have moved around the world over the last 400 years. In many places, they have taken the land and other resources from the native people. People from Europe, Asia and Africa started moving to the Americas in the 1600s. People are still going to the Americas today, but in much smaller numbers. The most popular destinations are Canada and the United States of America.

Around 1800, people started moving into Australia from Europe. There was also a movement of Han Chinese into areas of southern China around this time. In both cases, the original inhabitants lost land and often lost their lives. Disease, warfare and the changing environment all contributed to some populations growing and others shrinking. Many native people were forced to move off their traditional lands.

World population

No one knows how many people had settled around the world 12 000 years ago. Maybe it was one million or as high as ten million. All we know is that population growth was slow for a long time. In the last century, this growth has increased rapidly.

In 1900, the world population was less than two billion people. In 1959 it reached three billion and in 1999 it doubled to six billion. By June 2007, there were almost seven billion people on Earth. Scientists estimate that there will be nine billion people by the year 2050.

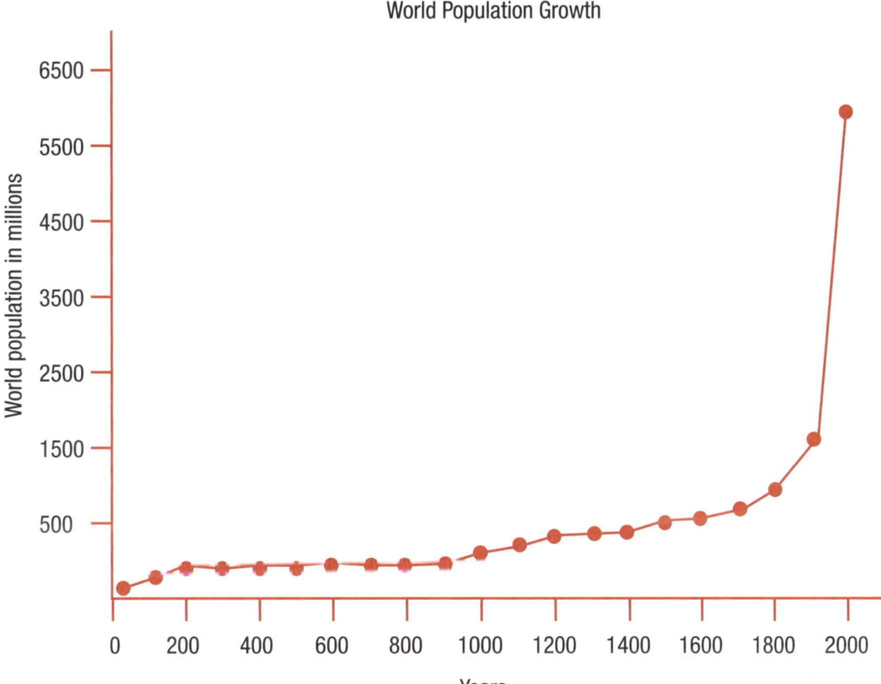

For you to try

- How does the graph look if you add nine billion at the year 2050? How long has it taken to settle the world?
- How quickly are settlements and world population growing now? What impact on the world does this population growth have?
- Consider the three parts of the biosphere and the impact the next two billion people will have. How many people can the Earth support? Can the population keep doubling?

Two things are now happening as populations grow. First, while the rate of population growth today is very rapid, it will be much slower in fifty years' time. Second, city populations are growing faster than rural populations as more people are moving to cities. This can make **population density** very high in some places. The largest cities of the world have very dense populations.

Urbanisation

Urbanisation happens when a settlement turns into a city. New cities are being made all over the world. Old cities are getting bigger, as rural people are migrating to cities. Cities like Tokyo and Yokohama in Japan start to run into each other. They are part of larger urban settlements. Another example of a large urban settlement is the area from Boston to Washington D.C. in the United States of America. New York and Baltimore are all part of this giant urban area.

The largest cities in the world			
Over 25 million people	**7–18 million people**	**12–14 million people**	**10–11 million people**
Tokyo, Japan	Mexico City, Mexico Mumbai, India Sao Paulo, Brazil New York, USA	Shanghai, China Lagos, Nigeria Los Angeles, USA Calcutta, India Buenos Aires, Argentina Seoul, South Korea Beijing, China Karachi, Pakistan Delhi, India	Dhaka, Bangladesh Manila, Philippines Cairo, Egypt Osaka, Japan Rio de Janeiro, Brazil Tianjin, China

For you to try

- Collect information and pictures on any of the big cities listed in the table.
- Compare the type of settlement you find with a city that you know.
- Compare living in a very large city to where you live. List the good and bad things about living in a big city, then discuss the values and attitudes your list shows.
- Tokyo and Yokohama have a total population over 32 million. Can you find these cities on a map?

Growing populations

Most population growth is taking place in the developing world. India and China both have populations of over a billion people.

New York, in the United States of America, can have a population of 25 million during the day and a population of nine million at night. This is because many people leave the city to go home after work.

People in Beijing, China.

Countries by population in the year 2000		Countries by population in the year 2050	
Country	**Population**	**Country**	**Population**
China	1 268 853 362	India	1 807 878 574
India	1 004 124 224	China	1 424 161 948
United States	282 338 631	United States	420 080 587
Indonesia	213 829 469	Nigeria	356 523 597
Brazil	175 552 771	Indonesia	313 020 847
Russia	146 709 971	Pakistan	294 995 104
Pakistan	146 342 958	Bangladesh	279 955 405
Bangladesh	130 406 594	Brazil	228 426 737
Japan	126 699 784	Congo (Kinshasa)	183 177 415
Nigeria	114 306 700	Mexico	147 907 650

For you to try

- What do these countries have in common? What makes them different? What types of groups can you put them in? What continents are they on?
- The populations for the year 2050 are estimates. What is an estimate? What could happen to change these estimates?
- How does the list change over 50 years from 2000 to 2050? Why might some countries have left the list? Why might some countries have joined the list? Why might some countries have changed position on the list?

World population density

The world population is not spread evenly around the Earth. It is hard to live in many parts of the biosphere. For example, Antarctica has no permanent settlements and very few people live in the Sahara Desert. Human beings have changed the face of the Earth. Human settlement and use of resources now has a growing impact on the land, the oceans and the atmosphere.

Approximate populations of each continent in 2002			
Continent	**Population in thousand millions**	**Population in millions**	**Population in billions**
Asia	3 776 000 000	3 776	3.776
Africa	832 000 000	832	0.832
Europe	727 000 000	727	0.727
North America	501 000 000	501	0.501
South America	3 57 000 000	357	0.357
Australia	20 000 000	20	0.020

Mawson Base, in Antarctica, is not a permanent settlement. Antarctica is the least populated continent on Earth.

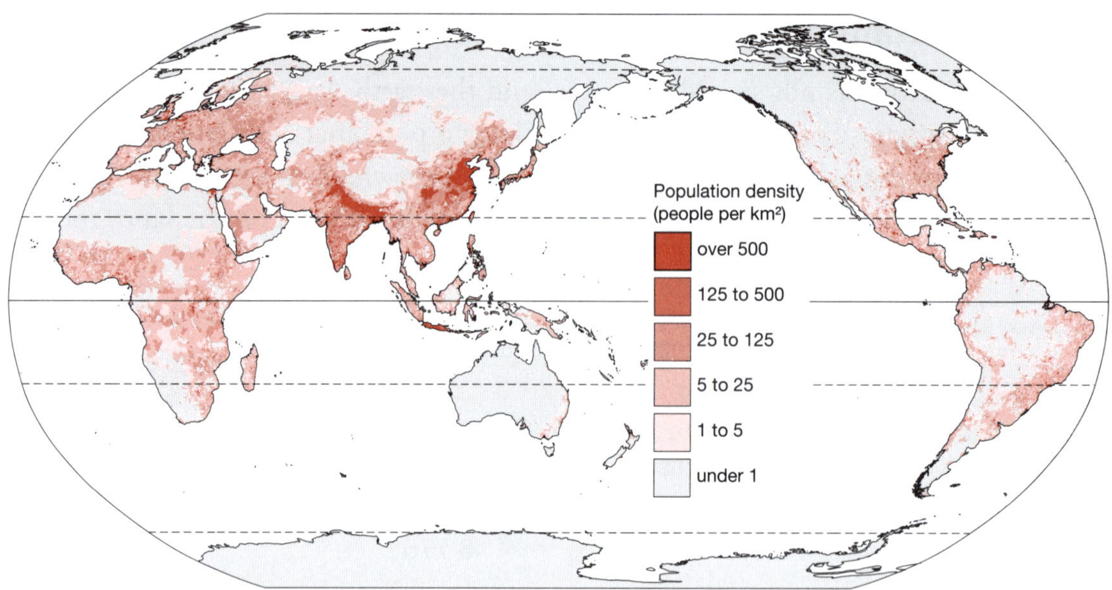

For you to try

- Look at this map of world population density. Light shading shows lower density. Darker shading shows high density.
- How does the map relate to the ten most populous countries?
- How does population density relate to the physical map on the inside of the front cover? How does the map relate to the climate zones?
- How does the map relate to the continents?
- What other things can you think of that the map relates to?

Adapting to the physical environment

Over the past 50 000 years, people have adapted to living in many different areas. They live in lowlands at sea level and high altitudes in the mountains. People have adapted to living in deserts with very little water. They live in swamps that are covered by water. They live in very hot places and very cold places. People have adapted to living in some of the harshest and most difficult living environments around the world.

The Tibetans live at elevations of 3 000 metres in Tibet. They have physically adapted to the low oxygen levels at these altitudes. They have 500 times more red blood cells than people living at sea level. They have large lung capacity and their bodies produce less lactic acid so that their muscles do not feel so tired when working.

People in deserts face dry heat during the day with little moisture. They keep their bodies covered to stop moisture escaping from their bodies. At night, temperatures can be extremely cold.

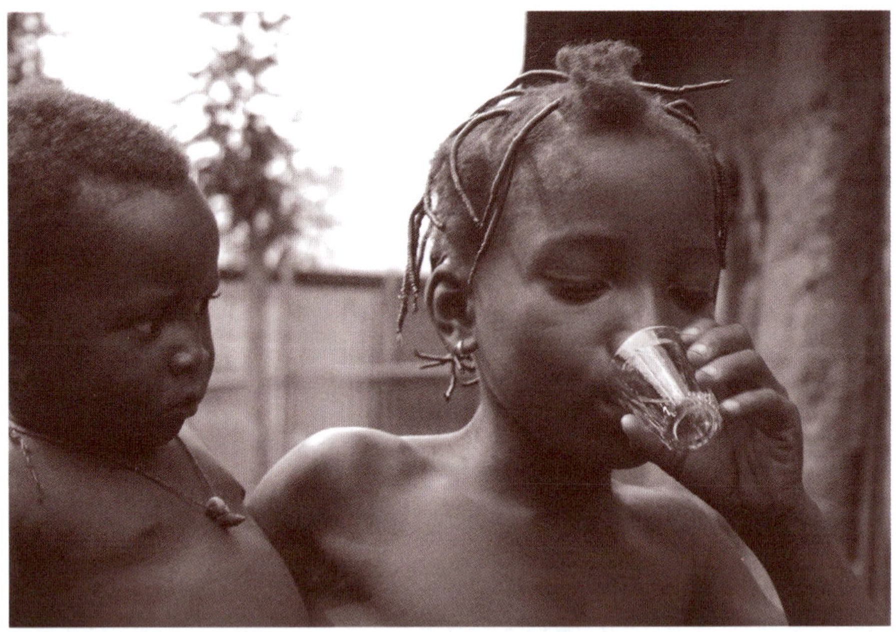

In the humid tropics, there is plenty of water and plenty of moisture in the air. People wear less clothing and their bodies are adapted to the hot humid climate. Growing populations make finding clean water harder.

In the Arctic regions, people need warm clothing and shelters. Their diet is rich in fats to keep their bodies warm.

For you to try

Discuss what you see in these pictures. Compare them with life in Papua New Guinea.

Natural resources around the world

People have become very good at taking resources from around the world. But all resources are finite or limited. They can be used up. The development of science and technology over the past 200 years has helped discover more resources. This lets people live better and helps populations grow – until the resources run out.

The Earth itself is our greatest natural resource. The total surface of the Earth covers about 510 million square kilometres. It is made up of two parts. The land covers about one third of the surface. Water covers about two thirds of the surface. This means that for every 70 square kilometres of water, there is 30 square kilometres of land. The air, land and water combine to create an environment that is good for human beings.

Air

Plant life in the oceans and on land produces the oxygen that we must have to breathe. But air pollution is a growing problem. Burning coal and oil for power causes much of the damage. The world needs more and more energy so we can drive cars and trucks, power factories, and heat and cool our homes. Air pollution is growing in China, Eastern Europe, Russia and Asia. This is also caused by burning land to clear it. (That has been done in Papua New Guinea for thousands of years.)

Air pollution, or 'smog', occurs in many big cities.

Water

Fresh water was a free resource for many people in the past. Today, safe drinking water is becoming scarcer as populations grow. In China, where the economy is growing very fast, water pollution is common. Rivers disappear as factories use up the water. They also turn into black streams of chemicals when factories put waste back into them. Lack of water is another problem in dry areas such as Northern Africa and Australia. In these areas, irrigation for agriculture is taking more and more water.

While it may seem that there is plenty of water on Earth, many places are becoming hotter and drier.

Land

The land holds our forests, deserts, and grasslands. It also holds other environments that contain natural resources. Vegetation makes up nearly all of the living matter on the land. One hectare of forest may hold up to 40 000 types of insects, and hundreds of different animals, trees and plants. Rainforests are home to very complex life forms.
So are coral reefs.

Rice, wheat, corn, and millet are some of the most important grains that people grow around the world.

The land produces food for us. About 15 per cent of the land is **arable**. It is used to produce seasonal crops like sweet potato, corn, grains, vegetables and fruit. Another five per cent is used for permanent tree crops. Over 40 per cent of the world's population is directly involved in agriculture. Two hundred years ago it was over 90 per cent. People are using natural resources more efficiently, so fewer people are needed for agriculture each decade.

Grazing land for animals is another important resource. In some places, forests are being burned to create more grazing lands. This is destroying one natural resource to create another. It causes great environmental losses and air pollution. Forest areas and wetlands are shrinking. Forests that provide wood and other products are being cut down. The wetlands are being drained. This leads to the **extinction** of animals and plants. It creates more erosion and flooding because there are no trees to slow water and soil run-off. Parts of Malaysia and Singapore are covered with smoke haze each dry season. This is caused by humans burning forests in Indonesia. Grassland soil is much thinner and less productive than forest soil. It is very hard to re-grow forests once trees have been removed to create a grassland.

Minerals

Minerals are natural resources that are taken from the Earth. Some countries have more mineral wealth than others. For example, most of China's minerals are in its territory of Tibet. Minerals are also found in the sea. And many mines are found in mountainous areas. The mountain chains running north to south in North and South America have many mines. Many mineral resources are **non-renewable**. Once a mine is empty it must close. These resources are quickly being used up.

For you to try

Take one mineral from the first list and one mineral from the second. How much information can you find on the two minerals? Compare their use, where they are mined, and their value.

Put these minerals into different groups after the class has discussed them. Explain how and why you have grouped the minerals differently. (Note, you can have more than two groups.)

List One	List Two
Petroleum	Lead
Copper	Zinc
Bauxite (aluminium ore)	Titanium
Coal	Lithium
Iron ore	Magnesium
Gold	Silver

Sustainable use of natural resources

The growing world population puts more and more pressure on natural resources. People everywhere are trying to improve their economies and lifestyles. This uses up more resources. Recycling and careful use of resources are two ways to help protect them. Improved technologies can also help sustain resources and find new ones.

Both the land and sea hold many life forms that we still do not know about. Science has recorded about one and a half million living species. But there may be another 28 million species still to be recorded. All are potential resources.

For you to try

Divide into teams. Each team can study a problem such as water pollution or air pollution. Search for information and organisations that work on this problem. What sustainable practices can you find? What other solutions can you find? Present your results to the class.

Renewable and non-renewable energy

There are many types of energy resources. The world economy needs energy resources to grow. Oil (petroleum) and natural gas are two very important fuels that provide energy for transportation on land and sea and in the air. Coal is another important natural resource that is used to create electricity. Oil, gas and coal have been produced over millions of years but they are not renewable – one day they will run out.

The oil industry started in the United States of America and helped to create the automobile industry. The United States came to depend on cars and trucks for transportation. But its oil supplies dwindled. Most of its supplies now come from the Middle East. The biggest oil producer is Saudi Arabia.

The United States, Russia, China, India and Australia all have much greater coal reserves, which could last for another 200 years. However, coal produces a lot of carbon dioxide when it is burned for energy. Coal is more damaging to the atmosphere than oil or gas. One solution to the problems caused by coal, oil and gas is to find cleaner renewable fuel resources.

Presently, the world still depends on oil, gas and coal for most of its energy. The biggest problem with alternative energy is the cost – the non-renewable fuels cost less. Currently, no one has to pay for the damage they cause to the environment or the carbon dioxide they release into the atmosphere, but this is now changing.

An oil well in Texas, United States of America.

For you to try

- Study one or two renewable sources from the following list to see how they can be used. Look at a world map to find places that offer suitable conditions for these resources.

Renewable energy source	Where and how it works	Problems
Hydro	Water power – water is collected in dams and used to drive turbines to produce electricity. (People used simple water power for centuries in water mills that ground up wheat and other cereals.)	Dams will eventually fill up with silt. They impact on stream flow and fish migration. People have to leave their land when construction of a dam floods it.
Solar	Sun power – solar panels can heat water and charge batteries but solar energy needs to become more efficient to produce a lot of power. (Plants have used solar energy for millions of years.)	The technology is still very new and works best in warm, sunny climates but not as well in colder regions.
Wind	Wind power – wind can be used to drive turbines in wind farms to produce electricity. (Windmills, like water mills, were used to grind grain for hundreds of years.) Denmark is a leader in this field.	Windmills need a constant supply of wind so wind farms may be situated far from where the energy is needed. Windmills can be a hazard for birds. They can be noisy and unattractive.
Bio fuels and biomass	Alcohol produced from crops such as corn and sugar cane to use as fuel – this is happening in some places like Brazil and the USA.	High-value crops are required so this process can be costly. In poor countries, there is the question of best use of the land for the nation.
Geothermal	Ground heat – the deeper you go beneath the surface of the Earth, the hotter it gets. Heated water from natural or introduced water sources can be used to drive turbines to produce electricity. New Zealand is a leader in this field.	Areas of the world where heated water is being pushed to the surface tend to be unstable. The technology is still experimental.
Tidal	Water power – in some places, the tide may rise three to four metres. This force can be used to generate electricity.	The technology is still experimental. Corrosion and storm damage are constant hazards of the sea.
Nuclear	Nuclear power – a proven technology that can produce power. It is used in the USA and Europe.	Nuclear power produces toxic waste that takes thousands of years to break down. Nuclear accidents can poison the environment and kill people. Nuclear technology may also lead to producing materials for nuclear weapons.

Natural disasters

There are many natural hazards in the environment, such as earthquakes, tsunamis, volcanic eruptions, floods, storms and fires. There have been many of these events in human history. Being prepared can help stop them from becoming large-scale natural disasters. For example, maybe people did not realise they had settled on a flood plain or did not know that they were living in an area that could be washed away by a tsunami. Often people know the risks but they do not make changes. Sometimes they cannot make changes. For example, they may not be able to move from where they live. Many disasters are a combination of natural events and human influences. This list shows some of the worst disasters that we know about. There have been many more, but they do not occur that often.

Place	Disaster	Year	Number of people killed
Bangladesh	Cyclone	1991	140 000
Japan	Earthquake	1923	143 000
Yellow River, China	Flood	1887	1 000 000
Portugal	Tsunami/earthquake	1755	60 000
China	Earthquake	1556	830 000

For you to try

Choose an event from the list. Find the country on a map.

- Why do you think so many people died?
- What is the hazard? What are the risks? What can people do now to avoid this hazard?
- In World War II (1939–1945) about 40 000 000 people were killed. How does that compare to the worst natural disasters we know about? What does this tell us about natural and human disasters?

Disease

Modern transport and trade can help to spread disease quickly. For example, many countries around the world are fighting new strains of bird flu. The World Health Organisation tries to help countries prevent contagious diseases like tuberculosis, malaria, HIV/AIDS and bird flu. This is a good example of international co-operation.

The hole in the ozone

The ozone layer is located in the **stratosphere**. It protects us from the sun's ultra-violet rays. These rays can be life-threatening. In the 1930s, humans began creating chemicals that started to destroy the ozone layer. In the 1970s, some scientists started to worry about the damage these chemicals were causing. In 1984, scientists found a big hole in the ozone layer above Antarctica. Governments around the world came together. They agreed to stop producing these chemicals. In 2007, scientists found that the hole was getting smaller.

Global warming

One of the biggest hazards that we face today is **global warming**. This is the heating of the Earth's atmosphere. It is caused by nature and by humans. Humans are speeding up this process by putting more **greenhouse gases** into the atmosphere. The greenhouse gases keep the Earth warm by holding in the sun's heat.

There are three major greenhouse gases:

- Carbon dioxide – this is created by burning forests, burning coal and oil for fuel, or using products such as diesel, petroleum and kerosene.
- Methane gas – this is produced by rotting vegetation. Cattle and humans are also major methane producers.
- Water vapour – this occurs in the form of clouds.

What is a greenhouse? A greenhouse is a glasshouse used to protect plants from the cold in temperate climates. The glass traps sunlight to keep the plants warm. That is where the name for 'greenhouse' gases comes from.

We need greenhouse gases to keep us warm. But they are making the Earth too warm, and this is affecting the land. Glaciers are starting to melt. Scientists worry that parts of the Greenland icecap, parts of the Arctic ice and some of the Antarctic ice will melt too. Melting ice will raise the level of the sea. Sea levels are rising by about 20 millimetres every year. Scientists are afraid that this rate may increase. Many low-lying coastal areas will face flooding and storm damage as the sea rises. Millions of people might have to move from coastal locations around the world. For example, much of Bangladesh and island nations such as Tuvalu and Kiribati will be **submerged**.

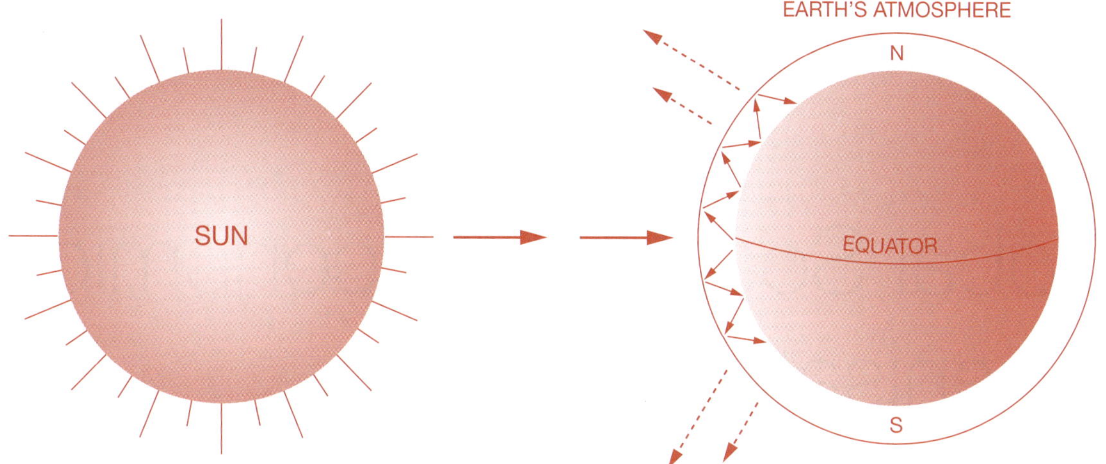

Greenhouse gases trap some of the sun's rays. The more gas there is, the more rays are trapped. This increases temperatures.

Global warming will make seawater more acidic, affecting marine life. It will heat ocean waters. The warmer waters will heat more air. This will make stronger storms and cyclones. A similar process will happen on land.

The solution is to reduce the amount of greenhouse gases people are putting into the atmosphere. Scientists hope people can put less carbon dioxide (CO_2) into the atmosphere. Carbon dioxide makes up 70 per cent of all greenhouse gases. Governments around the world will need to come together like they did to help preserve the ozone layer. Many nations have already started to work together. An international meeting in Japan developed the Kyoto Protocols. This is a set of guidelines to help prevent global warming.

Polar bears hunt seals on the ice in the Arctic. As the ice melts more rapidly, some polar bears are being forced to swim long distances to find food. Some move into urban areas to forage for human scraps.

2 Global Social and Economic Organisation

Chapter summary

In this chapter you will have the opportunity to:

✓ look at governments and economies around the world

✓ learn how governments have changed throughout history

✓ study international relations and co-operation

✓ identify social changes and issues of world progress.

Syllabus references

Strand: Organisation

Sub-strand: Social and Economic Organisation

Outcomes

6.2.1 Students are able to identify and describe the form and origin of contemporary, traditional and constitutional government in other parts of the world.

6.2.2 Students are able to outline conditions that have led to the present day international forms of trade and government.

6.2.3 Students are able to suggest changes to trade and government that would lead to social and economic development at the international level.

Governments around the world

Governments rule nations. The most accurate world political map would show the boundaries of about 268 nations, dependent areas and other bodies. Nations are the most common unit. The map on the inside back cover shows the larger nations in the world. You would need to use an atlas to find many of the smaller ones.

All over the world people live with different types of government. Most people live with several types of government at once. In Papua New Guinea there is local government, provincial government and national government. All of them have rules and laws. All of them provide services to people. Many other countries have similar levels of government.

Country	Local government	Provincial government	National government
Indonesia	Districts and villages	Regencies and provinces	Parliamentary democracy
USA	County, district	States and territories	Federal democracy
China	Banner, league	Provinces and autonomous provinces	Single party communist rule
Australia	Council, shire	States and territories	Federal parliamentary democracy
Myanmar (Burma)	Districts	Provinces	Military dictatorship

For you to try

Divide the class into four groups. Discuss the purpose of government with your group and present your ideas on one of the following topics:

- Government is who has the power to make and enforce the rules.
- Government is the organisation that provides services (roads, education, hospitals, water) and protection (police, army) for the people.
- Government is like an agreement between the people that some will rule and others will follow. The rulers will provide services and protection for the followers.
- Government is about who gets power and benefits in society.

Different ways to rule

There are many different forms of government. They include monarchy, democracy, theocracy, socialism, dictatorship, fascism and communism.

Governments are made up of different parts in order to rule a country. Often these three parts are called the three branches of government. The three branches of government in most nations today are:

- Executive – the nation's leader (the president or prime minister)
- Legislature – the law makers (parliament, senate, house of representatives)
- Judiciary – the justice system (judges, courts and magistrates)

Sometimes each part of a government is closely linked. Sometimes the three branches of government work separately. This is called the 'separation of powers'. It usually results in better conditions for the citizens of a nation.

The word part 'cracy' comes from Ancient Greece. It means 'government' or 'to rule'. Can you think of any other names for governments that end in 'cracy' besides democracy and theocracy? What is a bureaucracy? What would a 'studentocracy' be?

Parliament House is the seat of government in Canberra, Australia.

For you to try

- Which types of government do you know about? Give a definition and examples for each one.
- Why do you think it is good to separate the executive, legislature and the judiciary?
- What would happen if the president of a country also made the laws and acted as a judge?
- Can you think of a type of government where the executive, legislature and the judiciary are all the same?
- What examples can you find of the judicial branch of national governments?

What is a democracy?

The most common type of government around the world today is democracy. 'Demo' means 'people', so a democracy is 'rule by the people'. The United States of America is one of the oldest and most stable democracies. It represents over 300 million people. The largest democracy in the world is India. It represents over one billion people.

A direct democracy is where everyone votes to decide the rules. Direct democracy started in Ancient Greece over 2 200 years ago. This first democracy had few **eligible** voters. The only people allowed to vote were the free adult male citizens. (This was actually a **minority** of the population. The rest of the population was made up of adult women and slaves.) Small towns and villages may practise direct democracy today.

Voting in a democracy is an important role for all citizens. Most democracies today are 'representative'. This means that the people vote for a **candidate** who will represent them. The people might have a direct vote for the candidate they choose. Or they might have an indirect vote. For example, citizens in the United States of America vote for an 'electoral college' and the members of this group have a direct vote to choose the president.

The President of the United States of America lives in the White House, in the capital city of Washington D.C.

For you to try

- Why is it important for citizens to vote in a democracy?
- What branch of government sets the rules for voting?
- What branch of government decides if the rules for voting have been properly followed?

The number of candidates running for a position can make the voting process more complex. For example, ten people are running to be the president of a republic. The vote is very even, so a person with only 11 per cent of the total votes could win. That means that 89 per cent, or nearly all of the people, did not vote for the winner. This system is used in some countries. It is called 'first past the post'.

One solution is to have a second election between the two candidates with the highest number of votes. In the second election, the winner would get more than 50 per cent of the votes. This system is used in East Timor to choose the president. It is called a 'run off' system.

Another solution is to use voting **preferences**. For example, if there were ten candidates, then each citizen would number their choice from one to ten. That way a candidate can be chosen by counting the preferences. It is possible for a candidate who doesn't have the most first preferences to win. A type of this system is used in Australia.

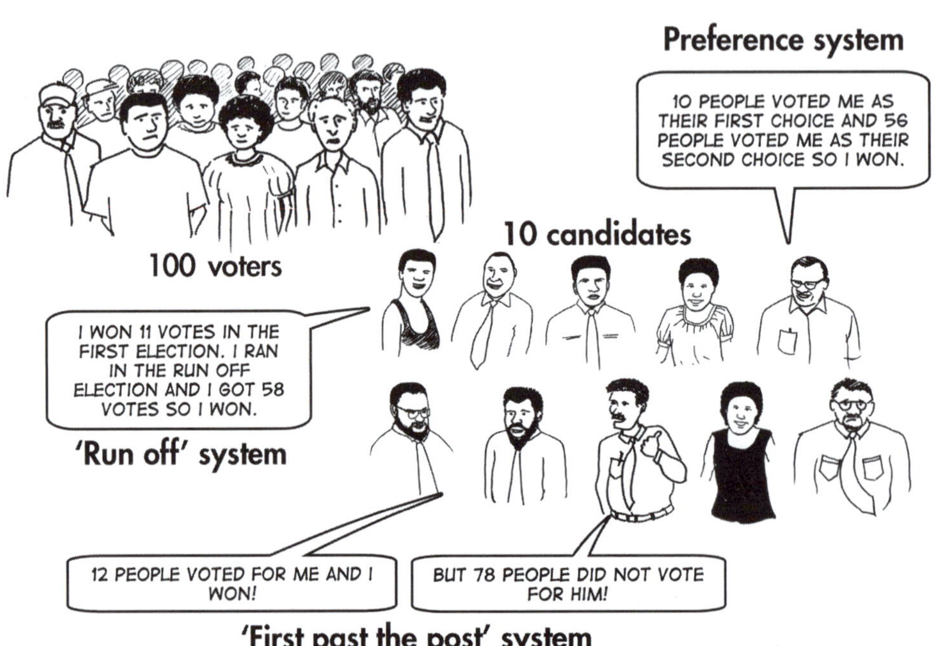

Democratic countries often use a system of boundaries to decide which candidates the citizens can vote for. For example, a country might have ten provinces. People in each province vote for a representative in government. But if one province has 1 000 people and another province has 100 000 people, is this fair?

One solution is to have two different groups of representatives for each province. For example, in the United States of America there are 50 states. Some are very large and some are very small. The legislature branch of the government is made up of two groups called the Senate and the House of Representatives. Each state elects two senators for the Senate. Some senators represent millions of people and some represent much smaller populations. Each state also has candidates for the House of Representatives but this number varies from state to state. States with large populations have more representatives than states with small populations.

Other democratic countries use a similar system. They have two groups or 'houses' for the legislature. This is called a 'bicameral' system. ('Bi' means 'two' and 'cameral' means 'a room'.) Other countries have only one group or house for their legislature, called a 'unicameral' system. ('Uni' means 'one'.)

For you to try

- Does Papua New Guinea have a bicameral or unicameral system of legislature?
- Does Australia have a bicameral or unicameral system of legislature?
- Why do you think some nations have one group, and others have two groups of representatives?
- What are the advantages and disadvantages of having one or two houses of representatives?

What is a dictatorship?

A dictator is a person who has all the power in a government. Dictatorships started in Ancient Rome around 2 000 years ago. The Roman Senate would appoint a dictator during a time of emergency or crisis. The dictator was given power over everyone else until the crisis was over.

There have been many dictators in the past century. Military dictators seize power by using the armed forces. In the past, many South American countries had long periods of military dictatorship. They include Paraguay, Chile, Argentina, Colombia, Peru, Ecuador and Venezuela. Today these countries are democracies.

Closer to Papua New Guinea, there have been long military dictatorships in Indonesia, Burma (Myanmar) and Thailand. Military dictatorships usually start with a coup. This is a revolution that removes the elected government. Fiji has had four military coups. Some small countries have no military forces to hold a coup. Larger countries like the United States of America, Canada and Australia have military forces but they have never had coups. Strong democracies do not have coups.

Military dictatorships usually do not separate the three branches of government. The dictator and his supporters can act as the executive, legislature and judiciary all at once. There is no one to check on them. They make their own rules. People cannot vote them out because there are no elections, or the elections are **corrupt**. Sometimes people have to fight to get dictators out of power. Sometimes the will of the people can force the dictator to leave without violence. In 1986, 'people power' in the Philippines forced the dictator to leave.

For you to try

- Which countries have military dictatorships today?
- Why is the military still in power in some places?
- Why are military dictatorships bad for human rights?
- Do small countries like Fiji need military forces? Why? Why not?

The people of Myanmar (Burma) live under military rule.

What is fascism?

The fascist system of government started in Italy in the 1920s. It quickly became another form of military dictatorship. A fascist government has power over almost everything in the nation. It controls business, commerce and industry. Fascism spread from Italy to Germany. The Nazi party became the most powerful fascist organisation in the world.

Fascist governments also started in Spain and Portugal. The German and Italian fascists tried to take over all of Europe and some other parts of the world during World War II (1939–1945). The Japanese military government joined them. They were all defeated in 1945, but the Portuguese dictatorship lasted until 1974. Germany, Italy, Spain and Portugal all have democratic governments today.

The National Socialist Party (or Nazis) came to power in Germany with only 40 per cent of the direct vote. Preferences gave them the majority. They declared an emergency dictatorship once in power. Their leader, Adolph Hitler, hated Jewish people. The Nazis murdered about six million Jews during World War II. Hitler committed suicide at the end of the war. The European Union was created to keep European countries together and stop wars in Europe.

Adolf Hitler started World War II. This was a disaster for Europe, costing millions of lives.

What is a monarchy?

A king, queen, tsar, tsarina, emperor, empress, shah and sultan are all **monarchs**. A monarchy is a system of **hereditary** rule, where the position of leader is inherited from the ruling family. Monarchies have existed for thousands of years. The position of monarch is inherited and passed down through 'royal' families, usually to the first-born son.

In the past, many people believed that kings and queens had a **divine** right to rule. They believed that their god had chosen them to rule. That belief is changing all over the world. Now more and more people believe they have a right to choose their own rulers. There are still monarchies around the world today but many have little or no power. England, Denmark and Holland all have democratic governments. There are still monarchs but the monarchs have no real power. The longest line of monarchs still in existence is the Japanese royal family. Today they are part of the Japanese democracy. Two small countries that still have powerful monarchies are Tonga and Lesotho (in southern Africa). The King of Thailand still has the moral power to influence some government actions in his country.

Queen Elizabeth II is the monarch of England.

For you to try

- How many monarchs can you find in the world today?
- Who do you think are the most important?
- What purpose do monarchs serve now?

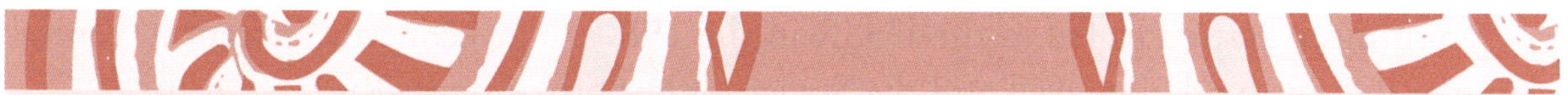

Sometimes governments can be very weak. They cannot maintain rules or law and order. Weak governments can become corrupt and they change often. They can also be targets for coups and military dictatorships. Portugal had weak governments for about 40 years starting in 1880. One government would stay in power until it was so weak that it changed with another one. This lasted until it changed with another one, and so on. These rotating governments lead to the name 'rotationism'. After rotationism, Portugal had a military dictatorship for 50 years.

What is communism?

In the communist system of government, the government owns all the land and almost all businesses. It is a type of dictatorship because there is only one political party. Communist governments can let people vote, but only for one candidate. Communist governments do not let people practise religion unless it is government-approved. The official communist belief is usually **atheism**.

The Soviet Union, or USSR, was the first communist government starting in 1918. Within ten years it became a severe dictatorship led by Joseph Stalin. He sent many people to prison and starved millions of farmers who rebelled against the government. He built many factories and created a powerful army that joined Germany in World War II. The German and Soviet armies attacked Poland. Then Germany attacked the USSR and eventually lost the war. Millions of Soviets were killed.

Joseph Stalin was a communist dictator.

Communism started to fail in the USSR in the 1980s. The economic system of central planning did not work very well and the Soviet Union broke apart. Russia and the Ukraine are the two biggest nations of the old union. There are many other smaller ones. All of them are trying different types of democratic government. But all of them face difficulties changing their economies.

China, Vietnam, Laos and North Korea are still communist countries today. But China and Vietnam are changing to a **market economy**. In these countries, there is still a single political party and the government is still a dictatorship. But some religion is now allowed. China now allows private ownership of land.

For you to try

North Korea is the last Stalinist communist government in the world.

- What information can you find about this country?
- What can you find about other communist countries? How are they changing?

What is socialism?

Socialism is an economic theory and type of government. A socialist government controls much of the land and production. It limits private enterprise. It is similar to communism because the government decides how the economy will work. However, there can also be socialist democracies.

Socialist countries can have very high taxes to share wealth. The heritage from the Swedish socialist system provides support to people from birth to death. No one will go hungry but the costs are very high. High taxes are used to provide education and medical services and a guaranteed income for everybody.

All modern democracies follow some socialist principles. They use taxes to share wealth. Some nations, like Australia, give more services and tax more. There are high taxes to support poorer families and farmers. Other nations, such as the United States of America, give less services and tax less.

For you to try

- What can you find out about the Swedish government? How can high taxes help more people have education and health services?
- What arguments can you find for and against socialism? What types of socialism can you find in Papua New Guinea?

A 'kleptomaniac' is a person who tries to steal everything. A 'kleptocracy' is a government that steals from the people. Some military dictatorships and some weak democracies can behave like this. A kleptocracy is very corrupt. It may collect taxes, bribes and other money, but the leaders and other officials keep this for themselves.

A kleptocracy provides very few services for the citizens. Many monarchies have acted like this in the past. This can lead to rebellion, coups and revolts.

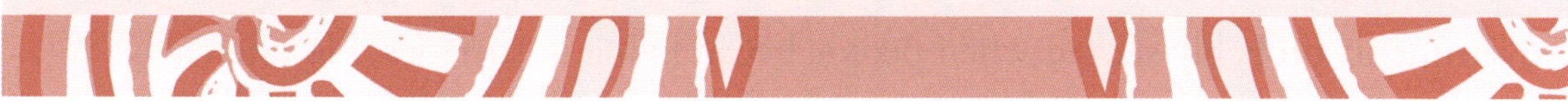

What is a theocracy?

'Theo' and 'deo' are both words for 'god'. A theocracy is a nation ruled by religious leaders. They interpret the word and rules of their god. Iran is a good example of a current theocracy. The religious leader, the Supreme Ayatollah, interprets the word of the Islamic god. The courts and laws are based on Islamic law. In ancient times, there have been many theocracies. There are **fundamentalist** Christian, Hindu, Jewish and Islamic groups today that would like theocracies based on their religion.

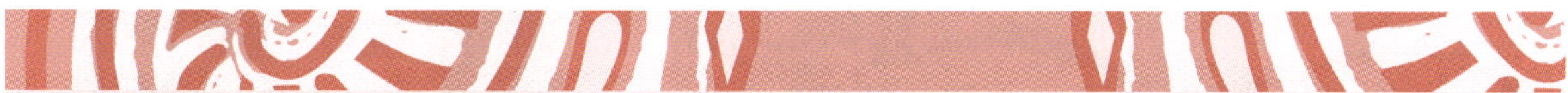

A 'constitution' is a set of fundamental principles and laws for a government. Constitutions can also give people rights such as freedom of speech, freedom of the press and the right to vote.

For you to try

- What branch of government changes or adds to a nation's constitution?
- What branch of government interprets the constitution?
- Why do dictators abolish or suspend constitutions?
- What is the value of a constitution for government and its citizens?
- What type of constitution would a theocracy have?

A Short World History of Governments

Every human settlement in the world has some history of government. Today we can find many different types of government around the world. Where did they come from? When we look at the distant past, we can see some general trends. We are only looking at clues. We can only guess at the whole story.

The first governments

Governments probably started when people began living in societies. No one really knows how long ago that was. It may have been over a million years ago with early humans, or 200 000 years ago, or 70 000 years ago.

The first simple systems of government probably developed in Africa amongst small groups of hunter-gatherers. Governments moved as people spread out across and beyond the African continent. Clues from **prehistory** show that some places had very important women as well as men in their governments. We don't really know how these governments might have worked. The leaders of these groups might have been warriors, hunters, religious leaders, or people who had special knowledge.

This cave painting was made by people in Europe about 30 000 years ago.

An early carving shows women played some important roles in prehistory.

For you to try

- What might these clues tell us about the way government worked for hunter-gatherers?
- What are the rules a hunter-gatherer society might need for its government?
- Who do you think the carved woman was? What values does she represent?

Agriculture and government

Agriculture started about 10 000 years ago. It allowed people to have permanent settlements such as villages. This made governments more complex. People had to protect their crops and make rules about land and irrigation. As crops, domestic animals and **irrigation** developed, settlements grew larger. They could support more people.

The area between the Tigris and Euphrates rivers was once known as Mesopotamia. It was called the Fertile Crescent. It used to be wetter and greener thousands of years ago. Modern countries in this region include Turkey, Israel, Jordan, Syria, Iran, Iraq, and Kuwait. Three great religions started in or near the Fertile Crescent: Judaism, Christianity and Islam. Governments have been fighting for power and land in this region from the earliest civilisations. Today it is known as the Middle East. It is a part of Asia.

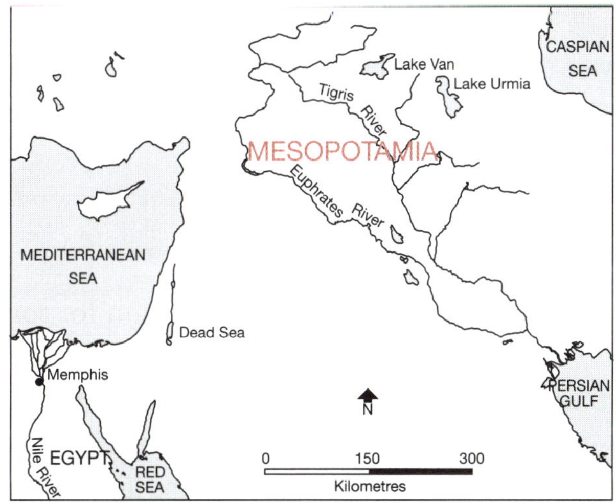

This map shows the Tigris and Euphrates rivers. 'Mesopotamia' means 'between the two rivers'. The first cities started here 5 000 years ago.

For you to try

Use a map to find the area that was once known as Mesopotamia.

- How many different ways could people and ideas come to this area? How might this location have helped cities develop?
- Why didn't the development of agriculture in the highlands of Papua New Guinea result in large cities? Did it result in more complex systems of government?

Divide into groups to see what information you can find on the governments of Turkey, Israel, Jordan, Syria, Iran, Iraq and Kuwait. Is religion still important to these governments?

Ancient Egypt

The civilisation of Egypt was based on the river Nile. Every year the Nile would flood, making the land very fertile and good for farming. But the problem was that the flood washed away boundary markers. People needed a way to tell who owned the different plots of land. A stable government helped maintain a system of land ownership. Like Mesopotamia, rules were needed to control irrigation too.

The words civic, civil and city are all based on civilisation. Cities are one marker of civilisations. Cities started in Mesopotamia first and in Egypt next. Both developed complex governments. The first Egyptian city was Memphis. Egyptian scribes developed **hieroglyphics** for writing. People are still finding and reading some of these today. The Egyptians also invented paper. This was made from reeds that grew in the Nile. But the Egyptian civilisation is most famous for its pyramids. They were gigantic tombs for kings and noblemen. Preserving the body for life after death was very important in the Egyptian civilisation. Egyptian **mummies** have lasted for thousands of years.

The Egyptian civilisation was a major power in the region for some 2 000 years. It lasted nearly 3 000 years. Sometimes there were periods of internal fighting and very weak government. But there were three different high points of Egyptian civilisation.

Old Kingdom	This started about 4 500 years ago and lasted for nearly 450 years before fighting and internal weakness ended this period.
Middle Kingdom	This started almost 4 000 years ago and lasted for over 300 years before internal fighting ended this period.
New Kingdom	This lasted for over 460 years and endured many periods of internal fighting. When it collapsed about 3 000 years ago, the great period of Egyptian civilisation was over, and Egypt later had foreign rulers including the Greeks and Romans.

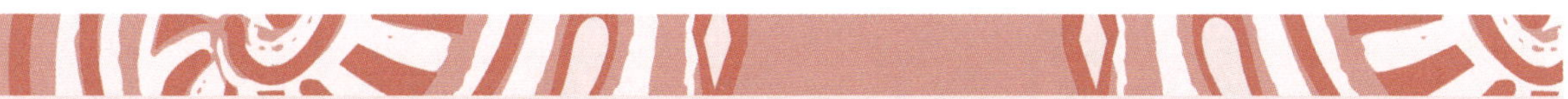

People still go to Egypt to see the pyramids. The first pyramids were built about 4 700 years ago. They are called 'step' pyramids. They looked like Mesopotamian temples called 'ziggurats'. Egyptians started smoothing and refining pyramids a hundred years after building the first step pyramids. They became bigger and bigger. The biggest is called the Great Pyramid. It is located at Giza.

The Great Pyramid was about 150 metres tall. It was made of limestone blocks that weighed over 1 000 kilograms each. People had to bring more than two million of these blocks down the Nile on barges and then transport them across the sand to build the Great Pyramid. It was built about 2 500 years ago. It took 20 years to finish.

Historians used to think that slaves built the pyramids. Now they believe that farmers and other artisans gave up their time to build these giant tombs. This is because people believed that the kings, called 'pharaohs', were gods. The Egyptians kept building pyramids for another 1 500 years after the Great Pyramid. But none were as big. Why do you think that might be?

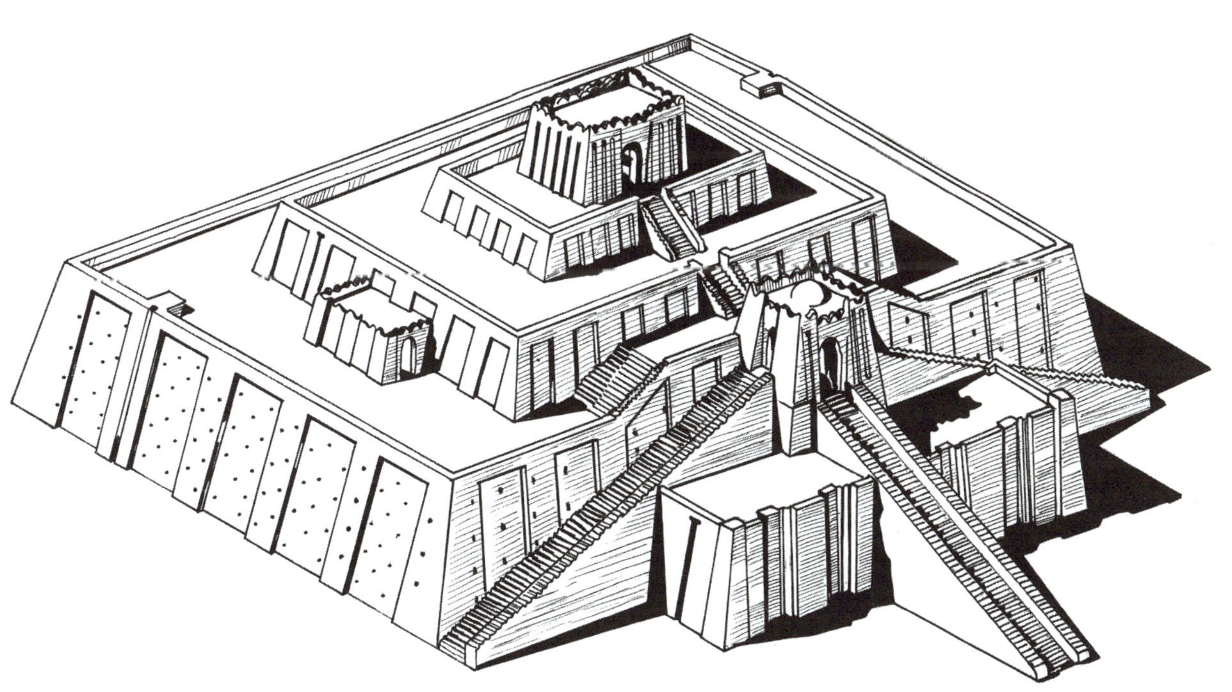

A ziggurat in ancient Mesopotamia.

The Great Pyramid at Giza, Egypt.

For you to try

- Why do you think Egypt was a great power and government for over 2 000 years?
- What is the situation in Egypt today?
- What do you think will happen to Egypt in the future?

City-states

The earliest civilisations became city-states. They had both urban and rural settlement. They had organised leadership and religion. The farmers grew wheat and barley, along with other foods and livestock. These grains can be stored for long periods of time, so this system provided **surplus** food. Extra food meant that not everyone had to farm their own food. They could take up trades (weaving, building, healing), study religion and astronomy, or join the armed forces.

Cities and civilisation spread or started in many other areas. They developed different types of government. They were often combinations of theocracies and monarchies. They supported large groups of priests or religious people. These people studied astronomy and the sun in order to improve methods of agriculture.

Ancient Greece and Rome

These are two of the most important early civilisations in Europe. The Greeks had a number of city-states. Ancient Greek citizens studied many of the ideas and sciences that later spread around Europe and other parts of the world. The different Greek states often fought each other. They also conquered parts of Asia and North Africa. The Ancient Greek civilisation extended as far as northern India.

The basis of the Greek economy was slavery. Eventually, when the Romans conquered the Greeks, some of the Greek slave owners became slaves for the Romans. The Romans used Greek knowledge to add to their own culture. They conquered much of Europe and parts of Asia. No one is sure why the Roman civilisation collapsed. But tribes from the north of Europe attacked and destroyed much of Rome in the year 410.

The Colosseum in Rome, Italy.

The Acropolis in Athens, Greece.

China

The greatest nation in Asia has always been China. There have been many other nations and smaller empires. For example, the Sri Vijaya Empire covered much of what is now Indonesia and Malaysia. And different kingdoms with rich cultures have risen and fallen in many other parts of Asia over the last 4 000 years. They include Burma, Cambodia, Thailand, Vietnam and the Indian sub-continent.

Ancient China, like Greece and Rome, developed many inventions and practical sciences. The south of China, like South East Asia, developed rice-based agriculture. The north developed wheat and other grains. Chinese agriculture goes back for thousands of years. The earliest Chinese city-states are found along the Yellow river and in the Yangtze valley.

The history of China is one of strong **dynasties** that helped unite the country. When one dynasty weakened, a new dynasty would take over. The last of the dynasties was the Qing dynasty. It ruled for over 250 years until 1910. In 1911 a republican government took over but it was weak. Warlords ruled in many places and later, the Japanese attacked China and occupied parts of it. The Communists took over in 1949 and have ruled ever since. Today China is a world economic power.

For you to try

- Can you find information about the Chinese government today?
- How does China today compare with Italy, the home of the Roman civilisation?
- How does China today compare with Greece, the home of the Ancient Greek civilisation?
- Why do you think that the three countries are so different?

Rice paddies in China.

Early civilisations in the Americas

There were many civilisations in the Americas before Europeans arrived. The Olmecs of Mexico developed one of the earliest 'new world' civilisations around 3 000 years ago. Mayan civilisation covered parts of Central America and Southern Mexico. The Mayans had their own system of writing and maths. They also had a very accurate calendar. Mexico City was the home of the Aztec civilisation when the Spanish arrived in the early 1500s.

In South America, the Spanish found the Incas in the highlands of the Andes. The Inca civilisation extended over thousands of kilometres. It covered parts of Ecuador and most of Peru and Bolivia. The Incas had a type of socialist society. Everyone was guaranteed food and people worked in teams on communal land. The whole team was punished if a person on the team broke the laws.

Today Mexico City is one of the largest and busiest cities in the world.

Machu Pichu in Peru is the site of famous Inca ruins.

Colonial governments

The age of European exploration began in the 1400s. Spanish and Portuguese **mariners** sailed around Africa to Asia. Christopher Columbus was the first European to sail to the Americas in 1492. By 1550, Spain and Portugal had colonised parts of Asia, North America, Africa and most of South America.

The European colonial age lasted from 1500 to 1945. Many different European countries claimed land for themselves on other continents. They established their own governments over the local populations. Sometimes they killed the people who owned the land. Sometimes they conquered them. Sometimes the colonists fought among themselves. The Dutch took colonies from the Portuguese in Asia. They also tried to take part of Brazil from the Portuguese. The British took New Amsterdam (New York) from the Dutch. The British and French fought over colonies all around the world.

The first American colonies declared independence in 1776. Others followed. Most of South America and Mexico was free by 1830. The French tried to colonise Mexico in the 1860s, but they were soon forced out.

Colonisation continued in Africa and Asia until World War II (1939-1945). The end of the war was the beginning of the end for most colonies. The French, British, Portuguese and Dutch all fought colonial wars after 1945. They tried to keep some of their colonies but only succeeded with some very small ones.

The colonial age is over. The colonising countries like Spain, Britain and France are not as powerful as they once were. An ex-colony, the United States of America is now a world super-power. Another ex-colony, India, is a growing power.

For you to try

Compare China, India and the United States of America.

- What makes them strong?
- What are their weaknesses?
- What can they learn from the past?

Globalisation

All nations on Earth have become closer over the last 500 years. The development of mechanical power during the Industrial Revolution (1769-1900) increased global production. This changed economies right around the world. We are now in the Information Age. Science and technology have helped industry. They have given the world powerful transport and communication systems that bring us all closer together. This is part of the process of **globalisation**. Globalisation connects people around the world with common products, ideas and experiences. Some people like the idea of globalisation. Others are frightened by it.

For you to try

- What evidence of globalisation can you find around you?
- What benefits does globalisation have for Papua New Guinea?
- What problems does globalisation bring to Papua New Guinea?

International relations

The 20th century was a period of many wars. Over 100 million people died in conflicts, including World Wars I and II. Wars were fought for human rights, national independence, trade issues, ownership of resources and religion. The League of Nations was formed after World War I to help prevent wars. But the United States of America voted against joining it. Later Italy, Germany and Japan all broke the rules and attacked other countries. The League of Nations broke down completely with the start of World War II.

The United Nations (UN) organisation was established at the end of World War II to help keep world peace. It started with 50 member countries in 1945. By 2007 it had 192 member countries. The United Nations is not a government body. But it supports many types of international relationships including:

- United Nations Development Programme (UNDP) – this helps developing countries around the world strengthen their society, government and economy.
- United Nations Educational, Scientific and Cultural Organisation (UNESCO) – this supports education, cultural development, cultural heritage protection, international cooperation in science, and freedom of the press.
- World Health Organisation (WHO) – this is dedicated to improving world health.

Countries around the world send their ambassadors to the United Nations headquarters in New York, United States of America, to have a voice in international affairs.

International Trade

International trade is important to every country in the world. But it is very complex, with many different rules and values. Some governments think that making money is the most important value. Others think that keeping farming families on the land is an important value. Governments have to make decisions about which values are more important.

The World Trade Organisation (WTO) meets with representatives from most nations. They try to improve conditions for world trade. The biggest problem is that every country wants to sell its products freely to other countries. But few of them want to buy other countries' products without protecting their own local businesses and farmers. They use **taxes** and **duties** to do this. They may also limit the amount of goods that can be imported. For example, Japan has placed a limit on the amount of beef Australian farmers can sell them each year.

Both the United States of America and Europe give their farmers **subsidies** for growing, or not growing, a particular product. Poorer countries cannot compete. They want free markets for their agricultural products but they also want protection for their industries.

Free trade or protection? These are the two opposite approaches for international trade. In 1776, tea and silver were important world trade items. The Scottish economist Adam Smith published a book called *The Wealth of Nations*. In this book, he argued for free trade and against protection. Here are some of the views Adam Smith wrote about.

First, the market of Europe has become gradually more and more extensive ...

Secondly, America is itself a new market for the produce of its own silver mines; and as its advances in agriculture, industry and population, are much more rapid than those of the most thriving countries in Europe, its demand must increase much more rapidly ...

Thirdly, the East Indies is another market ... [for America, the Portuguese, Dutch, English, French, Swedes and Danes] Even the Muscovites now trade regularly with China by a sort of caravans which go over land through Siberia and Tartary to Pikin ... The increasing consumption of East India goods in Europe is, it seems, so great, as to afford a gradual increase of employment to them all. Tea, for example, was a drug very little used in Europe before the middle of the last century [1650]. At present the value of the tea annually imported by the English ... amounts to more than a million and a half a year.

For you to try

- What food products and metals are important trade items today compared with 1776?
- What do you think the most important world trade items will be in the future?

The British colonies in America had started to revolt in 1776. They wanted the freedom to trade. They did not want to pay tax on tea imported through Great Britain. Then, as soon as the colonies became the free United States of America, they started protecting their industries. Back then, two of the most important trade items were tea and silver. Today oil is an important trade item. But the basic questions about free trade are still the same. Both Europe and the United States of America promote free trade. They both still protect agriculture as well. The World Trade Organisation is still debating these issues today.

For you to try

- Why do you think countries want to protect their industries?
- Why do you think countries want free trade for some products but not for other ones?
- What solutions can you think of? Will they work in a democracy?

International products

People have been trading and spreading products around the world for a long time. Today, many countries depend on international trade as an important part of their economy. Better transport, storage and communication all make trade easier. Almost anything you can think of is a trade item somewhere. Mangos, passion fruit, chillies and coffee were all brought to Papua New Guinea through international trade.

Passion fruit is a tropical vine that produces a fruit. There are several types; you may have seen a purple one or a larger yellow one.

Where did it come from? It first started to grow in what is now Brazil. People have probably been eating it for thousands of years. When the Spanish and Portuguese came to Brazil over 400 years ago, the flower of the fruit reminded them of the crucifixion, or 'passion' of Jesus Christ. (If you can find a passion fruit flower, look at the different parts to see if you can see what the Spanish saw.)

Where did it go to? The passion fruit vine has been spread all over the tropics and even to some mild temperate zones.

What is it used for today? Its main commercial use is for juice or fresh fruit. It is used in some desserts and people eat it fresh where it is grown.

Mango is a tropical fruit.

Where did it come from? It first started to grow in the foothills of the Himalayas in Burma and India. Mangos can grow at sea level and up to altitudes as high as 1 200 metres. The earliest evidence shows that people were cultivating mangos about 4 000 years ago. The mango is an important item in the Hindu religion and culture.

Where did it go to? The cultivation of mangos spread from India and Burma east to other parts of Asia and to Africa, especially the east and west coasts. In the last 200 years, the cultivation of mangos has spread across the tropics and subtropics. Mangos are found in all tropical countries today, and in some subtropical places.

What is it used for today? Modern markets see mangos travel to many countries and places where they cannot be grown. The fresh fruit market for mangos continues to grow. People can buy fresh mangos in Europe, North America and the southern parts of Australia. This is after the fruit has travelled thousands of kilometres to market. Other products use preserved mango. These include juices, pickles, preserves, dried fruit, tinned fruit and chutneys.

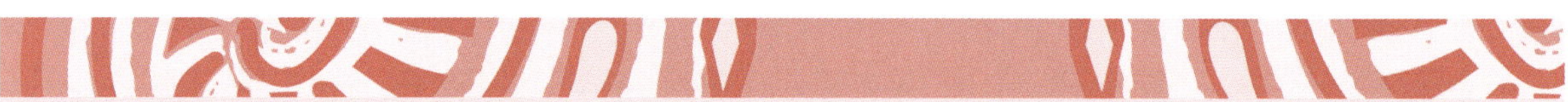

Chillies come from the capsicum species. There are various types. Some are very hot. They have also been called peppers (like the spice). For example, there are bird's eye chillies that are small and very hot. Then there are sweet chilli peppers (or bell peppers) that are sweet and mild. All of them are excellent sources of vitamin C.

Where did it come from? Chillies first started in South and Central America and in Mexico. People have been eating them for at least 9 000 years. First they took wild chillies and then started growing them perhaps as long as 7 000 years ago.

Where did it go to? Christopher Columbus was the first European explorer to travel to the Americas, in 1492. He brought chillies back to Europe. They have been grown in the warmer climates of southern Europe since 1500. The cultivation of chillies spread very quickly to Africa and Asia.

What is it used for today? Today fresh and dried chillies are very important for cooking in India, China, Thailand and other tropical countries. They continue to be important in the Americas. Sweet dried chilli powder is called paprika and spicy chilli powder is often called cayenne powder or cayenne pepper. Both are used in cooking in many parts of the world. Many curry powders have some chilli powder in them. Preserved and dried chillies are used all over the world in cooking. Capsicum spray is also used as a weapon.

There are two main types of coffee plants. Both are trees. Arabica coffee is a tree that produces a mild type of coffee. It is the most frequently grown commercial coffee plant. It grows best in highland or upland conditions with good soils. Robusta coffee is a bigger tree than the Arabica. It will grow in hotter coastal conditions where soils may not be as good.

Where did it come from? Arabica coffee originally comes from the highlands of Ethiopia. This is a country in northern Africa. Robusta coffee comes from the tropical forests near the Equator in Africa.

Where did it go to? Sometime between 1 000 and 2 000 years ago, Arabica coffee was taken to Arabia (in the Middle East) and then traded to Europe. Coffee-growing plantations spread to South America and the coffee trade grew. In the 1600s, coffee houses were popular places to meet friends and discuss events in many parts of Europe. Portuguese and Spanish colonists took the stronger Robusta coffee from Africa. It is now grown in Africa, and in parts of Asia and Brazil at lower tropical altitudes.

What is it used for today? The main use for coffee is drinking. It must be processed. There are different ways to prepare coffee from instant coffees to brewed coffees. Robusta is the major item in instant coffees. Other uses for coffee include flavouring for ice creams and other sweets. There are some coffee-flavoured alcoholic beverages too.

For you to try

Choose an international product (mango, chilli, coffee or passion fruit) and trace the history of the product on a world map.

- Can you find other products in your area that are made from some part of this product?
- How many ways can this product be used?
- Are there stories or traditions about this product in your area or family?

International trade includes **raw materials** like iron ore or dried chillies. It also includes processed products like stainless steel or chilli sauce. Usually, the more processing a product requires, the more value the end product has. A barrel of oil can be made into petrol, kerosene or diesel fuel. Or it can be used to make hundreds of other products like plastics, nylon or tyres.

Some countries process their own products. Others export the raw materials to other countries for processing. This may be because the market for the processed products is far away. The people may not have the expertise for this type of processing. And there may be labour shortages or labour might be expensive. Many countries do not have the money to process raw materials. They try to protect their workers by not letting processed goods into the country without adding taxes or duties. Many countries have quality standards that imported products might not meet. Very high standards keep many products out.

For you to try

Imagine you are using chillies (from Papua New Guinea) to make chilli sauce to sell at home and to trade with the world.

- Who are your competitors? How big are their markets? Can you make the sauce cheaper than they can?
- What will you need to make the sauce other than chillies? (There are at least four different types of things, do you remember?)
- Once you have produced boxes full of bottles of chilli sauce, how will you transport, market and sell them?
- Will your chilli sauce meet the international standards to get it into other countries?
- How much do you think your chilli sauce would cost in Europe or Asia?

Tourism is a major form of world trade today. People travel to other countries for pleasure or business. Education and health are also growing world trade items. People travel all around the world to get university educations or medical treatment or to work in schools and hospitals.

Tourists travel to Uluru in central Australia. Tourism is important to the economy here.

A university education has become a world trade item.

Sometimes people think processed products are too expensive. They try to make their own. They might be successful. Or they might begin to understand why the products are expensive. For example, an East Timorese family thought that the price of coconut oil was too high. They decided to make their own. They had their own coconut trees and a big pot. First they collected coconuts, then they put the coconut flesh in the pot. They cut wood and added water to boil out the oil. They cut more wood and added more water all day long. Finally they had made almost a litre of oil by the end of the day. But they were very tired. They had burned a lot of fuel and used a lot of water. They decided it was cheaper to buy the oil because fuel was scarce.

For you to try

Divide the class into teams to debate the following topics:

- A country must protect its workers and jobs by stopping cheap products coming in from overseas *versus* People prefer to buy cheap overseas products that are expensive to make in their own country.
- It is important for a country to try to sell its products overseas *versus* It is better to make everything in your own country.

Review

This chapter has covered a lot of material. We have looked at different types of governments. We have looked at how governments have changed over many years. We have looked at changes in population over time. We have seen how people around the world became more connected over time. We have looked at some of the problems in world trade. We have looked at international relations and international co-operation. We have seen how people have tried to stop wars and other violent conflict in the world.

Unfortunately there are still wars. There still is conflict. People and organisations are still working for world peace, fair trade and human rights for all the people of the world. These are very important goals. Sometimes it seems that not much progress has been made, but this is not true.

Case study: the slave trade

One of the biggest changes to government, society and trade in the last 200 years is the end of slavery. For at least 5 000 years, the slave trade was an important part of the world economy. This started to change in the 1800s. Now it has been stopped, or **abolished**.

Slavery still exists in some parts of the world but is now considered a crime against **humanity**. Most countries fight hard against it. Different forms of slavery existed right around the world but we will look at the situation in the Americas.

Indentured servants

When the Europeans first settled in the Americas. there were not enough free settlers to do all the work. People used prisoners, **indentured servants** and slaves to do work in the colonies. The Spanish used native populations in the highlands of South America as workers. But disease killed many native peoples.

The practice of indentured servants goes back to ancient times. Free people could sell themselves when European settlement started in the Americas. They were called indentured servants or bonded servants. They could sell themselves for seven or 15 years. They could even sell themselves for life, which is the same as being a slave. Very poor people had to do this. The treatment of these people was bad. The masters could punish their servants with beatings and whippings. About half of these European indentured servants died in the first two years of service in the colonies. In Virginia, in the United States of America, they were used the same as slaves to grow tobacco. In 1618, the government of Virginia gave landowners an extra 50 acres of land for each new indentured servant brought into the colony. This was government policy to build the economy.

Slaves

Perhaps 12 million Africans came to North and South America as slaves. This practice started with the Spanish and Portuguese in the 1500s. At least 100 000 African slaves came to Brazil in the sixteenth century alone. Slaves were needed to work in the sugar cane plantations that became very important in the 1600s. Cuba, Brazil, Colombia and Venezuela all had large slave populations to work in mines and plantations.

The first African slaves to come to North America arrived in 1619. The slaves were needed for the tobacco plantations in Virginia. There were many revolts. At first, indentured European servants and African slaves revolted together. The colonial governments worked to divide the two groups by colour. They used **racism** to keep slaves and indentured servants apart. They made different laws for white and black people. They improved the laws for indentured servants but kept harsh laws for slaves.

For you to try

In North America, people used Hebrew law from the Bible (Old Testament, Deuteronomy, Chapter 15 verses 12–15) to pay indentured servants when they had finished their term. Look these verses up in the Bible.

- Why do you think people did not apply this law to African slaves? Can you find any other references to slaves and 'bondsmen' in the Bible?

Slaves were used for labour in European settlement of the Americas. Many slaves were not happy. Who would be happy as a slave? There were revolts and revolutions by the slaves.

For example, a runaway slave named Zumbi became a hero to slaves in Brazil. He led a revolt and was finally executed by the colonial authorities in 1695.

The first successful 'new world' slave revolt was in Haiti. This is an island in the Caribbean. It was a French colony. The fight for freedom started a little over 200 years ago. The Haitian War of Independence started in 1791. Thousands of slaves started to burn down the plantations and kill the French people who ran them. The war lasted until 1803. A brilliant leader, François Dominique Toussaint L'Ouverture, led Haiti against the English, Spanish and French. After his death, the war became very cruel. The fight was between the Haitians and French troops who belonged to Napoleon, a great leader in France. The French troops started killing any black people they could find. The Haitians fought back viciously. Yellow fever, a deadly disease, probably killed more troops on both sides than anything else. Finally Napoleon's troops had to give up. Haiti's slave revolt created the second independent nation in all of North and South America.

Captain François Dominique Toussaint L'Ouverture played the French, English and Spanish against each other in his fight to free Haiti from slavery.

For you to try

- Do you know which was the first independent nation in the Americas? What happened to the slaves there?
- What can you find out about Haiti today?

For a long time, governments tried to keep the policy of slavery. Change was difficult. Slavery was not very profitable but the culture of slavery and racism was hard to change. Great Britain was the first colonial power to outlaw slavery in the early 1800s. Brazil was one of the last American nations to outlaw slavery in the 1870s.

Civil War

From 1861 to 1865, the people of the United States of America fought a civil war. The Unionists, based in the north, wanted to keep the country together. They fought the Confederates, based in the south, who wanted to keep slavery and separate from the United States. More than half a million people died in this civil war. People fought for a belief. Both sides thought they were right and the other side was wrong.

The Union won the war and the slaves were freed. The Thirteenth Amendment to the American constitution forbids slavery. In 1868, the American government added the Fourteenth Amendment to the Constitution. This said that all individuals born or naturalised in the United States are American citizens, including those born as slaves. This guaranteed all former slaves were citizens and had the rights of citizens.

A REWARD OF 5 OR 20 DOLLARS

Five Dollars will be paid for the apprehending of my negro man named Stephen, who, in looking out for a master from the 20th ultimo, has not returned to his duty, nor has he been heard of; is about 5 feet 8 inches high, stoutly built, well formed, speaks good English, and is inclined to be plausible; black complexion, small whiskers and a few white hairs in them. He is well-known about the city, has a free wife at Mr. Robert Anderson's market in King street. A reward of twenty dollars will be paid for proof to conviction that he is harbored by a white person or free person of any color.

A reward will also be paid for the apprehension of old limpy negro Fortune who for two months has been looking for a lost turkey. For further particulars inquire at the corner of St. Philip and Six streets.

J. JOONIS.

FOR SALE NEGROES

Joe, 50, competent butler.

Silvia, 35, excellent cook.

Charles, 21, Waiting man.

Sophia, 14.

The above family is well worth the attention of those wishing trusty negroes. They are to be sold to a city owner. For further particulars apply as above at 24 BROAD STREET, Old State Bank.

For you to try

- How important is the abolition of slavery?
- Why did people change their minds about slavery after thousands of years?
- Why does having the right of citizenship matter?

In Australia, Aborigines did not get complete citizenship until 1967. What problems do you think they might have had without citizenship?

Civil Rights

Even with citizenship, many African Americans could not vote for a hundred years after the American Civil War. Protests for civil rights started in the 1960s. Martin Luther King Jr was a great African American leader. In 1963, he was put in gaol for protesting against racism in the southern states. From his cell, he wrote a public letter about non-violent civil disobedience. Soon Martin Luther King Jr led a demonstration of about 250 000 people. They wanted jobs and equal rights for African Americans. They marched in the capital city of Washington D.C.

Martin Luther King Jr's most famous speech was called 'I Have a Dream'. Here are some quotes from this speech.

… Now is the time to rise from the dark and desolate valley of segregation to the sunlit path of racial justice.

In the process of gaining our rightful place, we must not be guilty of wrongful deeds … We must forever conduct our struggle on the high plane of dignity and discipline. We must not allow our creative protest to degenerate into physical violence.

I have a dream that one day this nation will rise up … live out the true meaning of its creed. We hold these truths to be self-evident that all men are created equal.

I have a dream that my four little children will one day live in a nation where they will not be judged by the colour of their skin but by the content of their character.

I have a dream today.

Let freedom ring.

And when this happens, and when we allow freedom to ring, when we let it ring from every village and every hamlet, from every state and every city, we will be able to speed up that day when all of God's children, black men and white men, Jews and Gentiles, Protestants and Catholics, will be able to join hands and sing in the words of the old negro spiritual, 'Free at last, free at last. Thank God Almighty, we are free at last.'

Protests continued in the southern states where governments had blocked rights for most black people. Some churches were burnt down and bombs killed some protesters. Some people resisted, but many started to change. The government passed the Voting Rights Act in 1965. This made it easier for southern African Americans to vote. The struggle for civil rights continued. Unfortunately Martin Luther King Jr was shot and killed in 1968.

For you to try

- If Martin Luther King were making his speech today, how do you think he might change it?
- Do you know of any other minority groups in the world today? Do they have civil rights? What type of dreams do you think they would make speeches about?
- Try writing a speech for a minority group.

Slavery today

There still is some slavery today even though it is illegal. No government in the world has laws for slavery. All government laws are against slavery. In some places the laws are not well enforced and there is some slavery. It is illegal. World organisations have made great progress in stopping most of it.

For you to try

Compared with 100 years ago:

- What are other areas of progress in the world?
- Where are lives better in the world?
- What is needed now for better international relations between countries?

3 Global Culture

Chapter summary

In this chapter you will have the opportunity to:

✓ identify and describe the basic features of some other cultures far from Papua New Guinea

✓ discuss similarities and differences in these cultures

✓ identify cultural changes around the world.

Syllabus references

Syllabus strand: Culture

Syllabus sub-strand: Cultural expression

Outcomes

8.3.1 Students are able to compare elements of other national cultures with our own.

8.3.2 Students are able to identify key elements that shape international culture.

8.3.3 Students are able to participate in international culture.

Culture around the world

In Year Six and Seven, you have looked at some cultures in Papua New Guinea. You have also looked at Melanesian, Polynesian and other Pacific cultures. Now you can look at different cultures around the world.

Cultures spread and change. Language, art, technology – everything that people do reflects some part of their culture. Today we see cultures mixing everywhere. We also see people dividing and fighting because of cultural and economic differences.

Let's look at some of the different cultures around the world. Indian, American, Chinese, Polish, Latin and Samoan cultures are all different national cultures. Cultures are different just like people are different. Respect for difference is important. No one should ever be ashamed of their culture.

Remember, all cultures are changing. Today, all national cultures are being influenced by other cultures. People in some places try to stop this. People in other places encourage mixing cultures and ideas.

For you to try

- Look at the physical map of the world to make a list of features that might influence world cultures. How many features can you find? How might they influence cultures?
- Look at the political map of the world. How would you use this map to divide countries into cultural groups?

What is culture?

Culture is just about everything that groups of people have or make. It includes:

- group beliefs and values
- attitudes
- ways of doing things
- roles and relationships
- responsibilities
- things that are made (for example, pencils, pants, dresses, houses, roads, and everything made by humans).

Almost everything you can think of is part of human culture.

Culture can be divided into thousands of types across the world. You could study culture all your life. You will be influenced by different cultures all your life. And you can watch cultures change and mix all your life.

Remember that you have your own local culture. Your local culture is part of Papua New Guinea national culture. Papua New Guinea national culture is part of Melanesian culture. Melanesian culture is part of Pacific culture. And Papua New Guinea and the Pacific share in many other cultural influences from all around the world.

The same is true for students like you from other parts of the world. Every person on Earth is now affected by more than one culture.

For you to try

Draw a simple picture of a man and a woman. Look at the following list of objects:

bamboo comb	coconuts
cotton singlet	dark glasses
kina and toea currency	lap lap with Papua New Guinea designs
nylon short pants	pandanus mat
radio	running shoes
sweet bun	string bag
towel.	

Add each object to your drawing. For example, give the man a pair of nylon short pants. Label the culture for each object in your drawing. Choose the cultures from the list below:

- your local culture (originally made and designed in your local area)
- Papua New Guinea national culture (originally made and designed in Papua New Guinea)
- Melanesian or Pacific culture (originally made and designed in Melanesia or the Pacific Islands)
- world culture (spread from one place and now common all over the world)
- other cultures that you know of.

Now discuss the pictures with the class. Some objects may belong in several cultures. You can continue to collect pictures from newspapers and other places. Label them and keep them on a wall in the classroom where you can study them.

When did culture start?

Human culture might have started with language. Or maybe it started with families. Or maybe it started with decorations. These things all started millions of years ago.

Decorations may be some of the earliest physical items of modern human culture. People may have used flowers and feathers as decorations. Or maybe they created scars and tattoos. We will probably never know. The first known beads were made from seashells by early humans. They are between 100 000 and 135 000 years old. Scientists found them in Algeria and Israel. Scientists have also found stone tools that are even older.

Agriculture provided an important step in human culture. Figs may be one of the first food plants cultivated in the Middle East. Seedless figs must have human help to reproduce. Small seedless figs that are over 11 000 years old have been found in Jericho. (This city in the Middle East is mentioned in the Bible.) Agriculture allowed cities to be built. Cities are an important source of culture. Today more people live in cities than ever before. Cities are a place where culture can change quickly.

Globalisation and cultural change

Cultures have always changed. This is true from the beginning of culture to today. Globalisation affects the way that cultures are changing. Ideas and experiences are becoming global. That means the same ideas and experiences affect people all around the world. Movies, radio, tourism and advertising have made some products global; for example, soft drinks, fast food restaurants and clothing such as jeans.

For you to try

- What items of global culture can you find in Papua New Guinea?
- Do you know where they originally come from?
- Can you tell how they have been adapted to Papua New Guinea culture?
- Does global culture have more influence in rural or urban cultures?

What is world culture?

World culture is what the people of the world have in common. The first main category of things the people of the world have in common is physical items such as televisions, radios, newspapers, books, movies, shoes, computers, clothing, pencils, chalk, cars and trucks.

The second main category of things the people of the world have in common is systems that are bringing people closer together. There are systems that let people understand more about each other. There are systems that let people share the same values, attitudes and beliefs. There are systems that bring the people of the world into closer contact. For example:

- transportation systems that let people travel around the world by air, sea, road or rail
- trading systems that allow trade items, money, credit (and debt) and tourism to move around the world
- communication systems that provide news, entertainment and direct human contact (the Internet, the World Wide Web, television, radio, newspapers and movies)
- religious systems that seek to influence more people around the world.

The third main category of things the people of the world have in common is beliefs and ideas. Sometimes the beliefs are strong and sometimes they are not so strong. Here are a few examples of beliefs and attitudes that are becoming more common around the world:

- wearing a tie shows respect
- human rights are important and people have a right to be free (except criminals)
- having winners in the Olympic Games is very good, and even if you cannot have winners, it is important for a country to have people compete
- hamburgers and fried potatoes taste good
- going to school and getting an education is important
- having dark glasses makes you look good and protects your eyes.

Things we have in common

Look at the pictures on pages 85 to 92. These pictures show some parts of different cultures around the world. How many things in the pictures do you also have in your area or in Papua New Guinea? Divide into teams. Which team can find the most things? Discuss how these things are part of world culture.

Systems we have in common

Look at the pictures on pages 85 to 92. Can you see evidence of systems? How many things in the pictures are part of a system that you have in your area or in Papua New Guinea? Discuss the ways that the systems in the pictures are connected to systems in Papua New Guinea.

Beliefs and ideas we have in common

Look at the pictures on pages 85 to 92. Can you see evidence of attitudes and beliefs? Do you know of similar attitudes and beliefs that people have in your area or in Papua New Guinea? Discuss some of your attitudes and beliefs that might be shared in other parts of the world.

The spread of culture

Cultures spread and travel across the world. There are many ways for culture to spread. Education systems spread national and international cultures. Governments may help to spread culture in other ways. For example, China's government is trying to make sure that every home in China has electricity, a television, a telephone and access to a road. The idea is to make national Chinese culture accessible to everyone. This also works to spread parts of world culture.

For you to try

Consider what the Chinese government is trying to do.

- How are telephones part of world culture? How is electricity part of world culture? How is television part of world culture? How are roads part of world culture?
- What connections can you see between world culture, world economic development and the world environment?

Some parts of world culture push people apart, rather than bringing them together. People use weapons to fight each other. International trade systems now allow more and more people to get weapons. The military **arms** industry is a big part of international trade. It can create conflict. Sometimes, religion and other beliefs can also divide people and create conflict.

For you to try

- Discuss the attitudes and beliefs you might not share with other people.
- Is world culture bringing us together?
- Is it pushing people and groups apart?

What makes culture

The table on page 93 shows some of the important things that make up a culture. It does not show all of them. You can see that all cultures have some things that are the same. For example, shelter is something that every culture has. There are many different types of shelter. But people can recognise shelter, even when it is very different from their own.

For you to try

- How many different types of shelter can you think of from around the world?
- What different types of shelter can you find in the pictures on pages 85 to 92?
- Why are shelters different? What does that tell us about different cultures in the world?

Other things that make up cultures can be very different, but serve the same purpose. Sometimes different cultures share the same thing, but they may use it differently. For example, English is spoken in Australia, England, the United States of America and Papua New Guinea. These countries all have different cultures. They speak English differently but all of them can understand each other (usually).

The human face and body is a recurring theme in the arts. What do you think the purpose of these items is? How do these objects compare with the arts in Papua New Guinea? What makes something art? How do you know if something is art or not? What is the purpose of art?

Different cultures treat death in different ways. What do you think about these pictures? What are some different cultural attitudes to death? How do ceremonies help the dead? How do ceremonies help the living? Different religions also have different kinds of ceremonies and cultural icons. What kinds of cultural expressions can you see in these pictures? Is there a relationship between religion and art? How do these pictures compare with religion in Papua New Guinea?

There are families all around the world. Families have many special cultural traditions wherever they are. What do these pictures tell you about families? How do families strengthen cultures? How do families change cultures? How does your family compare to the families in these pictures? What parts of Papua New Guinea culture does your family participate in? Do different cultures have different roles for men, women, boys and girls? How is this changing around the world? Can you compare the roles you see in these pictures with roles for men, women, boys and girls in Papua New Guinea?

These pictures show classrooms in Tibet and Colombia. Tibet is a colony of China and the students must learn Chinese. Colombia was a colony of Spain and Spanish is the main language. How important is education to culture? What type of education do you think these students are getting? How do these pictures compare with your own classroom?

These pictures show examples of the Chinese, Greek and American English languages. What can you tell about language from these pictures? What do these pictures tell us about global culture?

'Pop' culture, or popular culture, is found all around the world. In Mongolia people buy plastic flowers. The statue shows Paul Bunyon, a popular folklore figure in the early American timber industry. The third picture shows an Australian fashion model. What do these pictures tell you about popular culture? How do they compare with popular culture in Papua New Guinea?

Sub-cultures, or minority groups, contribute to larger cultures around the world. How important is it to keep some of the traditions of minority cultural groups? How do the groups in these pictures compare with minority groups in Papua New Guinea?

More than half the total world population now lives in cities. More people are migrating to urban settlements every day. Urban settlements have many modern cultural features like entertainment, transport, medical services, schools, universities and offices. How do the cities in these pictures compare with the cities in Papua New Guinea? Why do so many people want to live in cities? How do cities affect global culture?

Rural settlements create very different cultural landscapes. For example, a settlement on the Tonle Sap lake in Cambodia, a settlement in the volcanic mountains of Flores Island in Indonesia, and an African village. How do people adapt to living in rural environments? How do these settlements compare with rural areas in Papua New Guinea?

These pictures show food shops in Asia, Central America and South America. Food values, preparation and consumption vary all around the world. How is food important in different cultures? How do these markets compare with food stalls in Papua New Guinea?

Shelter is important in all cultures. These pictures show houses in Mexico, Switzerland, China and Ireland. What are the purposes of these houses? Why are they so different? How do these houses compare with houses in Papua New Guinea?

Sport brings many nations and many cultures together. These athletes are in a parade after the Olympic Games in Sydney, Australia in 2000. Some sports, like baseball, are more popular in some countries than others. How does sport bring people from different cultures together? What values can sport add to a culture?

Work is a big part of cultures all around the world. People must work to survive but there are many different kinds of jobs. How is work different in rural and urban settlements? How does work in Papua New Guinea compare with the jobs in these pictures?

What makes culture		
Arts (painting, music, literature)	Houses or shelters	Rural settlements
Death ceremonies (rituals and other practices)	Language	Sports
Popular culture, popular arts, fashion and entertainment	Marriage, separation and family relationships	Sub-cultures, special groups or associations
Education	Food	Urban settlements
Gender	Religion	Work

For you to try

Use the pictures on pages 85 to 92 to find examples of the different categories in the table. Think about the information in the first two chapters of this book.

- What cultural differences can you find for the different categories in the pictures? Can you explain some of the differences that you find?

Choose a country or region that is not in the Pacific region.

- What information can you find about this country for each category in the table? Can you find pictures (not in this book) to illustrate the categories? (If not, draw some of your own.)

Choose one category from the table and think of a few examples. (For example, if you choose 'Sports', think about cricket, baseball and basketball.)

- How many countries do you know that share this example? How many countries do not share this example?

Organise the categories in the table into groups. Explain how you have organised the groups.

- What other parts of culture can you add to the table or to your groups? Can you find groups that are not in the table?
- How do some categories in the table overlap? (For example, what about people who work in religion?)

Culture by continents

There are many ways to look at culture. We will try a few of them. We can only look at a few small parts of cultures because they are so rich. First, we can look at culture based on place, or location. For example, what cultural regions do the continents cover?

African cultures

The African continent covers two large cultural areas. North Africa shares much with the Middle East. There are Arab cultures and people have adapted to living in a dry environment. There is a long history of using written language and making urban settlements.

Southern African cultures are famous for the drumbeat and musical forms that have spread around the world. Southern African cultures value speaking and singing. They use bright colours just like bright music.

The African cultures brought many types of music to North America. Blues, jazz, soul, rock and roll, rap and hip-hop are all based on African cultural traditions. Slaves brought many musical forms to South America. The results include tango, rumba, samba, mambo, bossa nova, salsa and reggae.

For you to try

- Can you find any part of African cultures in Papua New Guinea?
- What comparisons can you find between North Africa and the rest of the continent?
- What do the pictures on pages 85 to 92 tell you about African culture? What is missing?

Choose one country in Africa and see what you can find out about its culture.

Southern African dancers in a colourful ceremony.

European cultures

Modern European culture is one of growing unity. The people of Europe are trying to work together more and more. They are trying to change a culture of conflict to a culture of co-operation. Europe is often now called a 'tolerant' culture. This means it allows differences. It supports democracy and human rights.

Europe is also famous for painters, architects and other artists. It has a rich physical culture and history. Much of this is kept in museums and galleries. The cultural history is also seen in buildings and landscapes.

Europe reflects a mix of cultures. Northern Europe with countries like Germany, the United Kingdom, Sweden and Norway, reflect a different set of cultures. Protestant religions are a common cultural feature. Northern European cultures tend to be more reserved. They also have beautiful buildings, artworks and landscapes. In southern Europe, the Greeks and Romans provided the base for a number of European cultures. For example, Latin culture started in what is now Italy.

For you to try

- Can you find any part of European cultures in Papua New Guinea?
- How many different cultures can you find on the European continent?
- What do the pictures on pages 85 to 92 tell about European culture? What is missing?

Choose one country in Europe and see what you can find out about its culture.

The Trevi Fountain in Rome, Italy.

Latin cultures

Latin cultures started with the Romans. Latin was the language of the Roman civilisation. Today, no one speaks Latin as a first language. So no one is really sure how the Romans pronounced Latin. The Roman Empire adopted Christianity as the official religion about 1 700 years ago. The Roman Catholic Church is an important part of Latin culture today. The Roman Catholic Church used Latin in religious services until well after World War II. Even now, the Latin language is important in some church ceremonies.

There are languages that come from Latin in other parts of what was the Roman Empire. The Italian, French, Spanish, Portuguese and Romanian languages are all based on Latin. People who speak these languages share some parts of Latin culture.

In traditional Latin culture, the value of honour is very important to men. Women dress modestly. They cover their heads and shoulders when going to church. Traditionally, the woman's place was in the home while the man worked.

The arts, poetry, philosophy and history were all very important in traditional Latin cultures. For a long time, the Catholic Church was the major **patron** for art. Churches and cathedrals in Spain, Italy and Portugal were places where painters and sculptors could find work.

The Virgin Mary plays an important role in Latin culture. She is celebrated in many ceremonies and with special prayers.

North American cultures

North American culture started with the indigenous people. Settlers from other parts of the world started coming from 1500. People have come from Europe, Africa and Asia. North America is now a blend of cultures. The United States of America is a major part of this.

The culture of the United States of America influences the whole world. Hollywood movies, democracy and the automobile are some of the American cultural influences that have spread around the world. Sometimes this is called 'popular culture'. Television and radio have spread many American cultural ideas through music, dance and drama.

The United States of America and Canada also have elements of British culture because of their colonial history. For example, they both use the English language and their legal system is based on the British legal system. They have many other cultural inheritances. For example, the French colonial period is still important in Canada. French is a major language there. Pidgen French is also spoken in some pockets of the United States, where there were French colonies.

For you to try

- Can you find any parts of North American culture in Papua New Guinea?
- Can you find any North American influences in the pictures on pages 85 to 92?
- What do you think are the best and worst cultural influences from North America?

The Hollywood Hills in Los Angeles, California.

South American cultures

South America, Central America and Mexico are all parts of Latin America. Latin American culture is a mixture of Latin culture and 'new world' cultures. When the Spanish and Portuguese came to Mexico and South America, they found colourful civilisations. The first explorers to Mexico said that Mexico City was grander than any city in Europe of that time (about 500 years ago).

The Aztec civilisation in Mexico had huge pyramid-shaped temples, large homes and wide plazas. The Spanish tore down the temples and built churches. But they adopted some of the foods like chillies, avocados, corn and cacao.

The Inca civilisation in Ecuador, Peru and Bolivia had roads, places of worship, and a complex system of agriculture that used potatoes, quinoa (a high protein grain) and corn. Over time, parts of the Inca, Aztec and other native cultures blended into the colonial Portuguese and Spanish cultures to become Latin American culture.

Guitars and music are one important part of Latin American culture. There is also a stronger indigenous influence than in most North American cultures. There were many more indigenous people in Mexico and the Andes when the Spanish came. The Spanish mixed with these people. They adopted many of the foods, building designs and the use of plazas and straight streets that were all part of native cultures.

African slaves brought in other cultural elements such as music, xylophones, and traditional ways of singing and story-telling. The result was new types of music.

For you to try

- Can you find any parts of South American or Latin American cultures in Papua New Guinea?
- Can you find any parts of South American or Latin American culture in the pictures on pages 85 to 92?
- What other examples of South American or Latin American culture can you find?

Compare these examples to what is done in Papua New Guinea. Can you find any news items or articles about African Americans or indigenous people in North or South America? What can you tell about them and their cultures?

Asian cultures

Asia is a mix of at least five major cultural groups. North Asia is Japan, China and Korea. These countries share some values such as education and respect for teachers. And they have similar architectural styles. China has the world's largest population. Chinese food is now found all over the world.

Southeast Asia includes the Philippines, Indonesia, Vietnam, Burma, Laos, Malaysia, Brunei and Thailand. These countries have a rich mix of cultures. They have both Chinese and Indian cultural influences. The Phillippines has Latin cultural elements too.

The Indian subcontinent is another major Asian cultural area with rice-based agriculture. India, Bangladesh and Pakistan are the three major countries of this region. They are divided culturally between Muslim and Hindu influences. The Indian Hindu religion follows a **caste** system. This means people are born into social groups from low to high **status**. The Indian government is trying to help the lowest group, called the 'untouchables'.

The Middle East is part of Asia. It is an Islamic cultural area. It is divided into two main Islamic groups the same way that Christians can be divided into Protestants and Catholics. In the Middle East, the two main Islamic groups are Shia and Sunni. The Shias are based in Iran. Mecca is the most holy city for the Islamic religion. It is in Saudi Arabia. This is a Sunni country.

Central Asia covers part of western China, Mongolia and the various smaller countries like Kazakhstan, Uzbekistan and Afghanistan. Herding animals is still very important. Tribal loyalty and tribal fighting are still common.

For you to try

- Can you find any part of Asian cultures in Papua New Guinea?
- What are the most important influences from Asia for you?
- Can you find any parts of Asian culture in the pictures on page 85 to 92?

Australian culture

Parts of Australian culture can be seen in Papua New Guinea. Australian culture also reflects European and North American cultures. Australia also has indigenous culture from its Aboriginal heritage. There is still a divide between some Australians and Aboriginal people. Like North America, Australian culture now reflects many different migrant groups from Italy, Greece, the Pacific Islands, Asia and Africa.

Cultural icons

We can look at culture through cultural **icons**. An icon is an image or symbol. A cultural icon is a symbol of that culture or a part of the culture. It is something famous or easy to recognise. It tells us something about the culture of a people or place. This is another way to look at some parts of our world cultural heritage.

Do you recognise these cultural icons?

For you to try

- What meaning do you think these cultural icons have? What cultures do they come from?
- How can two icons be similar, but come from different parts of the world?
- How can a mouse become a cultural icon? Can you think of any other animals that are cultural icons?

Country or region	Icons
United States of America	Marilyn Monroe, apple pie, baseball, the American flag (known as 'the stars and stripes')
India	Mahatma Gandhi, sacred cows, the Taj Mahal, curry
China	The Forbidden City, the Great Wall of China, Confucius, Mao Tse-tung (or Zedong)
France	The Eiffel Tower, Paris, the Louvre, Notre Dame
Australia	The Sydney Opera House, kangaroos, Uluru (Ayers Rock), Qantas
New Zealand	The All Blacks (rugby team), sheep, Maori carvings

For you to try

Copy this table on the blackboard or a piece of paper. Discuss the icons and see if you can find pictures of them. Add a row for Papua New Guinea and list some cultural icons that you know about.

- Can you tell what all of them are? Can you add any more icons for these countries to the table?
- How much do cultural icons really tell you about a country or culture? What do they tell you? What don't they tell you?
- Can you locate the countries in this table on a map?

Religions also have icons. This is where the word comes from. Originally 'icon' meant 'an image'. For example, a buddha is an iconic image of the Lord Buddha, who started the Buddhist religion. Later, an icon meant an image of Christ or the crucifixion, from the Christian religion. Now the word includes much more. The way the use of this word has changed is an example of the way culture changes.

Mulitculturalism or the melting pot?

Many nations make a choice about how they save or change their culture. Some try to mix everyone from different backgrounds to create a new culture. Others try to keep different subcultures existing side by side.

A good example is the United States of America. The government policy has been to create 'a melting pot'. This means taking everyone from different cultures and turning them into Americans. All Americans share different parts of the culture, no matter where they come from. Speaking English, attending school, paying taxes, defending America and defending the American constitution are all a part of joining the melting pot.

The United States of America now has cultural influences from all over the world. This includes:

- Northern Europe – for example, Holland, Scandinavia, Germany, Ireland and England
- Southern Europe – for example, France, Spain, Portugal and Italy
- Asia – for example, China, Japan, the Philippines and Vietnam
- Mexico and other parts of Latin America.

Within this melting pot there are many subcultures that have their own parts. This is called multiculturalism. For example, some of the subcultures are:

- Orthodox Jewish communities in Miami and New York
- Chinatowns in many major cities
- Latino sections of towns, particularly in the southwest
- Little Tonga in Los Angeles
- African American neighbourhoods in many states.

All these subcultures still share much of the culture and also create parts of it.

For you to try

- What do you think is best – a multicultural or melting pot system?
- Can you have both systems in one country?
- What can you find out about the cultural policies of other countries like Australia, France or China?

Spreading culture through ideas

Another way to look at culture around the world is by the spread of ideas. Religion and language are two different ways to carry ideas.

Religion

Religion is an important part of culture around the world. Look at the graph of major religions. Remember that each major religion can be divided into different groups. For example, about half of all the Christians are Roman Catholics. Muslims, Jews and Hindus all have different groups or **sects** too.

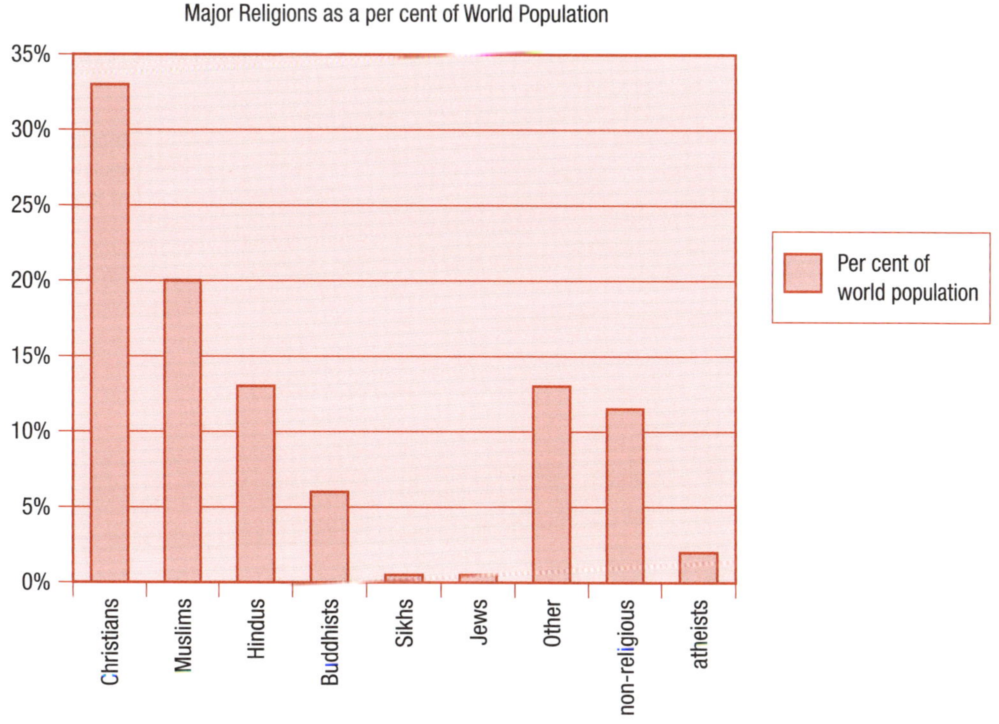

For you to try

Discuss what you know about the world's major religions.

- What information can you find about them?
- How do you avoid bias and prejudice in studying the world's religions?

Languages

There are about 3 000 to 4 000 languages spoken around the world. Look at the graph of the top ten first languages spoken in the world in 2004. They make up about 40 per cent of all first languages. This will change as world populations change. When language changes, cultures change too. For example, governments might promote one or two languages in schools so many smaller language groups are losing their language. Do you know of examples like this in Papua New Guinea?

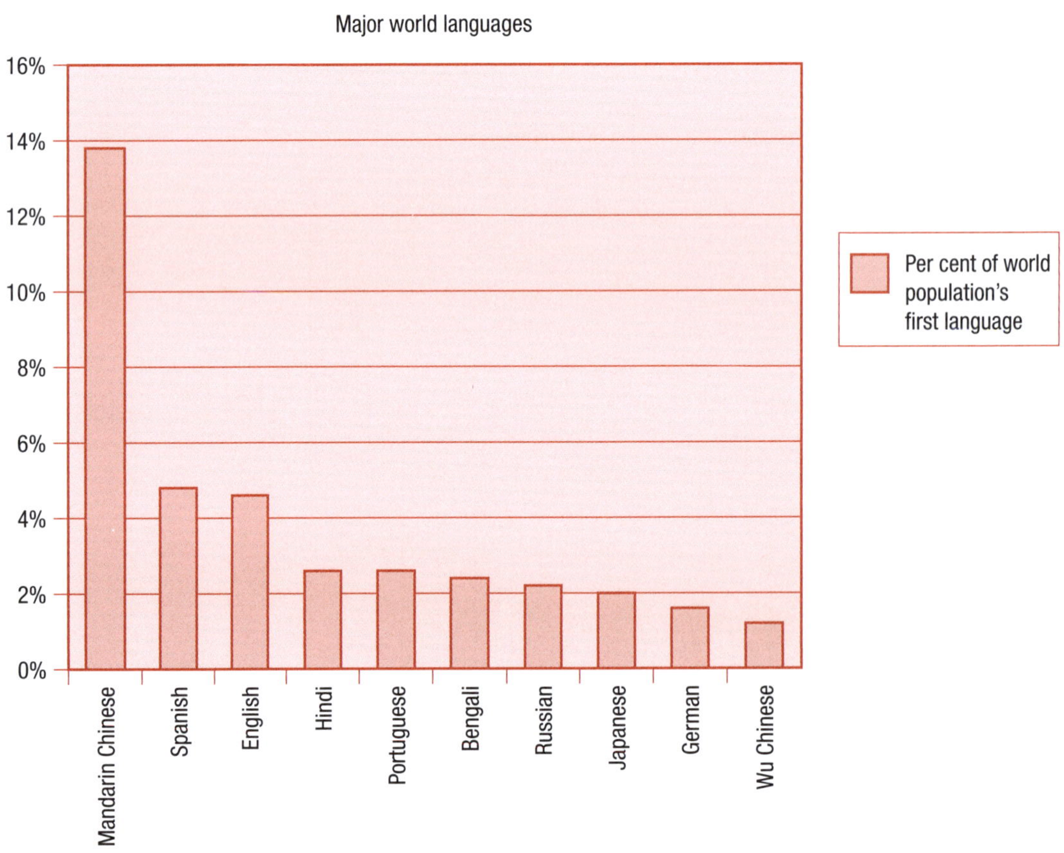

Some groups that share a language share some parts of culture. For example, English-speaking countries like the United States of America, Britain, Canada, Australia and New Zealand share some parts of European cultural heritage. There is a notion of fair play or giving a person a 'fair go'. They respect freedom of speech and the idea that a person's home is their private space. There are differences that have appeared over time, but there is much that is culturally the same.

For you to try

- How does language influence culture?
- What differences can you find in the different cultures that speak English?
- What changes have you noticed to languages that you know? How does it show that cultures are changing?

Culture wars

Different belief systems have caused conflicts. In the United States of America and many other countries, there are two cultural views. Often they are in conflict. One is often called 'conservative'. It is against things like abortion, gay rights and divorce. The other is often called 'liberal'. It allows people more freedom of choice on these issues. Sometimes these two groups are divided by religion. For example, in Christian cultures, the conservatives are called conservative Christians or fundamentalist Christians. The liberals are called liberal Christians and freethinkers. The same general cultural divide can be found in other religious groups such as:

- conservative or fundamentalist Muslims and liberal Muslims
- conservative or orthodox Jews and liberal Jews
- conservative Hindus and liberal Hindus.

In almost all countries and regions, there are cultural splits.

For you to try

- Can you find any information on a conservative cultural group?
- Can you find any information on a liberal cultural group?
- What type of divisions can you find in Papua New Guinea?
- How is this different from the United States of America?

Cultural stereotypes

Around the world, different cultures see each other with **bias** and **prejudice**. Being part of different groups can result in cultural labels based on race, religion, age or politics. Often these are **stereotypes**. A stereotype is a very biased idea of a culture. For example, the idea that all Australians drink beer is a stereotype. Conflicts also lead to stereotypes in world culture. For example, many Israelis and Arabs have stereotypes of each other in the Middle East. The idea of race is a cultural idea. It is not a scientific idea. There are many world cultural stereotypes that have been created with prejudice and bias. Close examination shows they are all false.

War leads to stereotypes. This is how many Americans thought of the Japanese and Germans in World War II. Today Americans, Germans and Japanese respect each other. Few people believe the old stereotypes.

Cultural stereotypes around the world		
Germans are cruel	Where do you think this idea comes from? Do you think it could be the result of wartime propaganda? How do you know it is a biased value held by one culture against another?	Do you know of any similar stereotype in Papua New Guinea or the Pacific region?
Africans are lazy	Where do you think this idea comes from? Do you think it has anything to do with slavery?	What other cultures have you heard called lazy? Have you ever heard young people being called lazy? Are young people a culture?
Scottish people are penny pinchers (they keep their money just for themselves and don't like to spend it)	Where do you think this idea comes from? What is the bias? What is the prejudice?	Are there stereotypes in Melanesian culture for people who don't share or give generously?
Australians are arrogant	Where do you think this idea comes from? What is the bias? What is the prejudice?	Who else have you heard this said about? Why is it a stereotype?
Americans are 'loud-mouths'	Where do you think this idea comes from? What is the bias? What is the prejudice?	Do any groups in Papua New Guinea suffer from this stereotype?

The opposite of sterotypes is an appreciation of cultures. Different cultures have developed wonderful ideas and systems. These are reflected in physical culture. Pages 109 to 116 show some of the beauty of different cultures around the world. This is a world heritage of culture. It belongs to all of us.

Stopping cultural change

In some countries, the government has policies to stop cultural change. They want to protect their own culture from the influence of other cultures and world culture. The communist government of China only allows 20 different foreign movies into China for public viewing at cinemas each year. It also worries about movies made in China. It fears some movies might influence people the wrong way. In North Korea, the government does not allow the people to see movies or books made in other countries. The government is trying to control culture and ideas. In France, a special committee meets to protect the French language. Shops and advertisers must only use French words. They are not allowed to use foreign terms. The French language has to be used in all schools. But some schools now teach English to get international students to come to France.

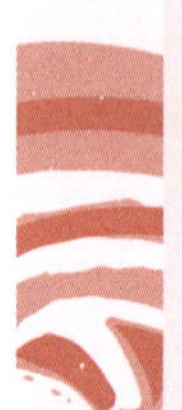

For you to try

- Which is stronger – a pure culture or a mixed culture?
- Like race, is the idea of a pure culture just a cultural invention?
- What part of your culture would you like to change or keep?

Culture and the Internet

The future of world culture is rapidly changing. The greatest new force for communication is the Internet. Access to the Internet is causing a cultural divide. People who have access can communicate with people all over the world. They can get information from all over the world.

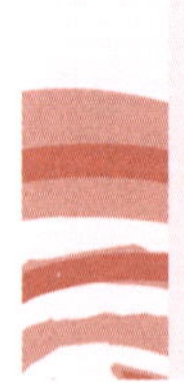

For you to try

- Who determines what a culture is or is going to be?
- How do you think the Internet will change world culture over the next ten years?

Global culture

Pages 109 to 117 show some of the special expressions of culture around the world. They are part of the cultural heritage we all share as humans.

Timbuktu, Africa.

Pyramids in Giza, Egypt.

Statues at Angkor Wat, Cambodia.

The Taj Mahal, India.

The Great Wall of China.

Potala Palace, Tibet.

The Sydney Opera House, Australia.

Statues on Easter Island.

The Acropolis, Greece.

The Eiffel Tower, France.

St Basil's Cathedral, Russia.

Stonehenge, England.

The Golden Gate Bridge, United States of America.

Quebec, Canada.

Statue of Christ the Redeemer, Brazil.

The Panama Canal, Central America.

Admiral Zheng was a famous Chinese explorer. He started exploring the world about 600 years ago. He had a large fleet of 300 ships with thousands of sailors. He explored parts of Southeast Asia and the East coast of Africa from around 1405 to 1433. The Imperial Government of China then stopped exploration. They thought that ideas from other countries were dangerous. They wanted to keep their own culture and way of government. They were looking inwards not outwards. If China had continued to explore the world after Admiral Zheng, how different might world culture be?

Europeans started their world explorations about 60 years after Admiral Zheng and his Chinese fleet had stopped exploring the world. European culture continued to change. It found new products and ideas all around the world. The Japanese did the same as the Chinese later in the 1600s. They stopped visits and trade with almost all other countries. They stayed looking inwards for 200 years. Then the Americans and British forced them to open for trade in the 1800s. This did change their culture and country very much. Today they have a much more open culture and a very strong economy. Do you think the two are related?

Admiral Zheng.

International culture

Read the following pages about some of the different parts of cultures in different places around the world. Compare these items and traditions to what you know about cultures in Papua New Guinea. Maybe you can find these items and traditions in newspapers and magazines. What does this tell you about the spread of culture?

Siesta

A siesta is a 'nap' or sleep that people have after lunch in Spain, Italy, Mexico and many other parts of Latin America and the Philippines. This tradition started in Spain. 'Siesta' comes from the Latin word 'sexta'. This means 'six' or 'the sixth hour of daylight'. After the sixth hour (or noon) you would eat and have a sleep. Then you would go back to work. People work until seven or eight o'clock in the evening in places where they have a siesta. Afternoon naps are common in other parts of Asia and Africa too.

Do you think this is a very good idea in places where it is hot at midday and in the early afternoon?

Piñata

A piñata (pronounced pinyata) is a clay pot that is decorated to look like an animal, a toy or a common object. It is filled with sweets. It is used at birthday parties in Mexico. The piñata hangs from a rope and children try to break it with a stick. Each child takes a turn. But they must wear a blindfold. That makes it hard to find and break the piñata. When it breaks, everybody tries to get the sweets that fall out. Now you can find piñatas for sale in Europe, Australia, the United States of America and Canada.

What customs do people have in Papua New Guinea to celebrate a child's birthday? How traditional are they?

Hamburger

The hamburger comes from the United States of America. No one is sure how this hot sandwich first started. It is made up of a fried minced beef patty inside a bun. It can have tomatoes, onion, lettuce and other foods with it. Large commercial restaurant chains started making hamburgers in the 1950s. Other chains followed with fried chicken and other foods. But hamburgers started the large-scale 'fast food' business. Today there are many well known hamburger chains. Some people believe that this reflects American culture taking over other cultures around the world. It is part of globalisation.

What do you think about the international spread of 'fast food'? Does Papua New Guinea have traditional fast foods too?

Carnivale is a special tradition. It is an important time for feasts and fun in many Latin cultures. Carnivale is two weeks of celebration before the more serious holiday of Easter.

Mardi Gras is part of Carnivale. 'Mardi gras' means 'Fat Tuesday' or 'Shrove Tuesday'. It is the last day for Catholics to eat meat before Lent. Lent is a time to prepare for Easter. Traditionally it is a time of 'fasting'. This means eating very little food. It is the opposite of 'feasting'.

Mardi Gras parades are celebrated every year in the city of New Orleans in the United States of America. It is part of the Latin culture of the city. It comes from when the city was first settled by the French in the early 1700s. Today, many people join in the Carnivale celebrations. The Latin culture has spread. Many of the people celebrating are not Catholics and do not have Latin backgrounds.

Many people go to Brazil to celebrate Carnivale.

For you to try

- Do you know any other special traditions that have spread from one part of the world to another?
- Where does Christmas come from? Where do New Year celebrations come from?
- Can you think of cultural times in Papua New Guinea where people fast or feast?

History and myth in culture

Myths and histories from different cultures give us many words and phrases that we use today. The phrase 'to burn your bridges' is thousands of years old. It comes from Ancient Rome. You might say 'Don't burn your bridges' or 'He has burnt his bridges' or 'She burned all her bridges'. 'Burning your bridges' refers to the Roman army general, Julius Caesar. He came back to Rome after conquering many lands. He crossed the Rubicon River and then he burned the bridge so that he and his armies could not turn back. Then he marched into Rome and took over the Roman Empire. When you 'burn your bridges' there is no going back. You must go forward, win or lose.

Julius Caesar became Emperor of the Roman Empire. Later, Roman Senators who wanted power for themselves killed him.

For you to try

- Can you translate the idea of 'burning your bridges' into your local language?
- Do you know any similar stories or phrases?
- Is 'do or die' the same as 'burning your bridges'?

Another phrase that is thousands of years old is 'Beware of Greeks bearing gifts'. This saying comes from the story of the Trojan Horse, from Ancient Greece. A horse is a large animal like a cow. The story of the Trojan Horse comes from a long war fought by the Ancient Greek army. They attacked a city called Troy. The city was surrounded by walls. But they could not get in. They tried for years to get inside. Finally, they built a large wooden horse. They hid some soldiers inside the horse. Then they pretended to leave. The people in Troy saw them go. They thought the horse was a gift. They pulled it inside the city. That night the Greek soldiers came out. They opened the city gates. The Greek army came inside and destroyed the city.

The wooden horse in the story is known as the Trojan horse. It was a bad gift. It looked good, but it brought death and disaster. People still refer to some gifts as 'a Trojan horse' today. It means something that looks good but will cause trouble.

For you to try

Sometimes an idea or a law can be described as a Trojan horse.

- Can you think of any examples? Have you heard any similar stories or phrases in Papua New Guinea?
- Can you find the country and story for each of these phrases from history, myths and legends? Sour grapes, Santa Claus, Pandora's box, a scapegoat, the Midas touch, a Benedict Arnold (or a Quisling), Achilles' heel, a red herring, sandwich, a flash in the pan.
- How far has each phrase or idea travelled? What other cultures use them? Can you find words in your local language, or in Tok Pisin, that come from these phrases or stories?

The Seven Ancient Wonders of the World

World culture is made up of ideas, systems and physical objects. Famous places and monuments are some of the easiest things to see. They have become part of world culture. Ideas about famous places have a long history. The Ancient Greeks are one group that started lists of famous places. They called them the Seven Wonders of the World. But remember that the world for the Ancient Greeks was just the Mediterranean region.

The original seven wonders were on a list of things for early tourists to see over 2 200 years ago. But it started the idea that we have a world cultural heritage. Today, the United Nations Educational, Scientific and Cultural Organisation (UNESCO) has a list that protects over 800 world heritage sites. Some of these are natural wonders. Some are made by people, like the original seven wonders. There is only one wonder from the original list still standing.

For you to try

Use a map or an atlas to find the homes of the seven ancient wonders of the world.

- What do you think the seven ancient wonders of Papua New Guinea might have been?
- What purpose did the seven ancient wonders of the world serve? What does this tell you about the ancient cultures of the Mediterranean?

Write a story or draw a picture that compares what you think was important in the ancient cultures of the Mediterranean and ancient New Guinea.

The original seven wonders were:

- The Colossus of Rhodes was a statue of a Greek god. Ancient Greeks built the statue about 2 300 years ago. It was 20 or 30 metres high. An earthquake destroyed it after about 50 years.
- The Great Pyramid of Giza was a tomb for an Ancient Egyptian pharaoh. The Ancient Egyptians built the pyramid over 4 500 years ago. It is the only one of the seven ancient wonders still standing.
- The Hanging Gardens of Babylon were a series of terraced walls and gardens. The Babylonians built them about 2 600 years ago. They were destroyed 600 or 700 years later by an earthquake.
- The Lighthouse of Alexandria was built by Greek rulers in Egypt about 2 300 years ago. It was over 100 metres tall. A fire burned at the top to light up the harbour. An earthquake destroyed it over 1 000 years later.

- The Mausoleum of Maussollos at Halicarnassus was a tomb for Maussollos. It was built over 2 300 years ago by Persians and Greeks. It was over 40 metres tall. An earthquake destroyed it about 500 years ago.
- The statue of Zeus was in Olympia in Greece. Zeus was the chief god in Ancient Greece and Olympia was the original home of the Olympic Games. The statue was built inside a temple about 2 400 years ago. It was an important religious site. It was over ten metres tall. It burned down about 1 500 years ago.
- The Temple of Artemis at Ephesus was built about 2 600 years ago by Greeks and Persians. It was for the Greek goddess Artemis. It took over 100 years to build. It burned down after 200 years.

Destroying world cultural heritage

An **arsonist** is someone who burns things down. Arson is a crime in Papua New Guinea. An arsonist burned down the Temple of Artemis. He wanted everlasting fame. People have destroyed other ancient and modern cultural sites on purpose. This might be for fame or for religious reasons or they might be insane. Destruction of cultural heritage often happens during wars.

The radical communist leader of China, Mao Tse Tung, ordered his people to destroy all their valuable ancient cultural items in the 1960s. Many statues were destroyed or defaced. This time was called the Cultural Revolution. But a better name for it might have been 'cultural destruction'. Valuable pottery, manuscripts and paintings were destroyed. Schools were closed. Teachers were sent to work on farms. Today the Chinese government protects the nation's cultural heritage and promotes education.

Early in the 21st century, the Taliban ruled in Afghanistan. They destroyed ancient Buddhist statues. The statues had been carved in a rock cliff and were over 15 metres tall. The Taliban destroyed them for religious reasons.

Another way that cultural items can be damaged is by being 'loved to death'. This happens when too many people come to see something and it may be damaged. For example, some people will write their names on ancient walls or pyramids. This is called 'graffiti'. The earliest example is from over 3 000 years ago in Egypt. People wrote their names on ancient monuments. This still happens today. It can cause damage.

Pollution can damage important monuments. Air pollution and acid rain are damaging famous statues and buildings in Europe, Asia and the Americas.

For you to try

- What destroyed most of the ancient seven wonders of the world?
- What are some of the dangers for world cultural heritage today?
- Do you think that human or natural hazards are the greatest danger to world cultural heritage?
- How is Papua New Guinea protecting its most important cultural items and places?

Protecting world cultural heritage

Museums are one way to protect parts of the world's culture. For example, the British Museum in London has sculptures from two of the original seven wonders of the world: the Mausoleum of Maussollos and the Temple of Artemis.

The United Nations Educational, Scientific and Cultural Organisation (UNESCO) World Heritage List protects many special places around the world. Each country has many more places that they want to protect. All countries try to protect their cultural heritage.

For you to try

Look at the pictures on pages 109 to 116.

- Are they 'modern' wonders of the world? Are they cultural icons?
- How do they relate to what you have learnt in this chapter?
- What other pictures can you find to express parts of the cultures of the world?
- Can you locate these places on a world map?
- What special parts of culture do they tell you about?

Improving Global Societies and Communities

Chapter summary

In this chapter you will have the opportunity to:

- ✓ look at governments and economies around the world
- ✓ learn and use the social science process
- ✓ use a variety of sources to make a study about societies and communities outside Papua New Guinea
- ✓ compare Papua New Guinea to other places around the world.

Syllabus references

Syllabus strand: Integrating Projects

Syllabus sub-strand: Societies and communities

Outcomes

8.4.1 Students are able to use the social science process to describe another nation and propose ways for Papua New Guinea to contribute more to the region.

8.4.2 Students are able to use the social science process to describe an international society and to propose ways for Papua New Guinea to be more involved in international affairs.

Integrating projects

The purpose of this chapter is to help you complete an integrating project. You can select any of the materials covered in the first three chapters for your final project. Then you will see how the three chapters link together. You may do a study on another nation of the world. You may do a study on an international organisation. In your project, you can compare what is happening in Papua New Guinea with another nation or other parts of the world.

Remember the list you made of places you didn't know about? Maybe you would like to study one of these places now. Finding information can be difficult. You will have to become a social science detective. You will need to search for information and ask questions. You will need to listen to the radio, look at newspapers, look for books and talk to people about different parts of the world. Some of you may have other sources of information, too.

Remember that you can compare pictures of different places. This is another way to learn. What pictures can you find for your project? What do they tell you? Compare pictures from different places. Use the pictures in this book. What pictures can you cut out of old newspapers or magazines? Making drawings and diagrams will also be helpful.

The social science process

This is the third year that you are using the social science process. This time, you will use it to investigate and compare countries around the world. You can also use it to investigate world organisations.

The steps to follow for the social science process are:

- observation
- having an idea or making a question
- gathering information
- evaluating the information
- making conclusions
- further study or follow-up studies.

Observation

The social science process starts with observation. This means seeing and hearing. It can include reading and looking at pictures in newspapers and books. It can mean listening to the radio or watching television (if you have one). It can mean talking and listening to people from different countries, or people who have been to different countries. It can mean talking and listening to people from international organisations, or people who know about international organisations. You can make written notes. You can collect pictures and articles. You can make comparisons. What other ways of observation do you know?

Ideas or questions

From what you see and hear, you might get an idea or have a question. Many scientists call this a **hypothesis**. The idea or question is what you study. For example, you might read that Fiji has had four coups. You decide to compare the recent history of Fiji with events in Papua New Guinea. Why has Fiji had coups when Papua New Guinea has been free of coups?

Gathering information

Next you have to carefully gather information about your idea or question. You may already have gathered some information to make your question. For example, you try to find information about coups. Are coups related to the environment? Or the government? Or the culture? Or the history? What can you discover about Fiji and how can you compare this with Papua New Guinea? You can find some information on the radio and in newspapers or books. You can ask people, too. Remember to consider attitudes and values when you talk to people. For example, you might find some people who think coups are good. You might find some people who think coups are very bad.

Evaluating the information

You need to look carefully at the information you find. Remember to consider the attitudes and values of the people who give you information. For example, you might want to know what happened in Fiji before the coup? Why did it happen? How does this compare with Papua New Guinea? Remember to look for bias and prejudice. You must study different values. Your evaluation will be a written report.

Making conclusions

Now you need to make conclusions. You will study your written report. The last thing you will write for it is the conclusion. The conclusion will give your opinion or idea. For example, you need to consider:

- What has made Fiji and Papua New Guinea different?
- How can countries avoid having coups?
- How could Papua New Guinea help Fiji?
- Should it help?
- Can we predict what will happen next in Fiji and Papua New Guinea?
- Can we be sure there will not be a coup in Papua New Guinea?
- What can citizens do to stop coups?

A good conclusion takes time. The best idea is to finish your report. Wait two days. Re-read the report. Now write your conclusion. This will take good planning. Your conclusion will be weak if you write your report on the last day. It is better to make a work plan. Give yourself plenty of time.

Further study

Nations and international organisations are always changing. Conclusions can quickly change. There will always be a need to continue studying.

For you to try

- What is the social science process?
- How will you use the six steps in your final integrating project?
- How can you use the social science process to study another country? How can you use the social science process to compare Papua New Guinea with another country?
- What are international organisations? How can you use the social science process to study international organisations?

Remember, the secret is to choose a topic that you like. Find something that interests you. If you like it, you will do it. If you don't like it, you will find excuses to delay. Take time to think about what really interests you. What do you really want to know about? There are three chapters of ideas in this book. Be sure to find something that you like!

For you to try

- What is the secret of doing a good project?
- How can you have a good work plan?
- How can you do a good report?
- How can you make a good conclusion?

Choosing countries and organisations

Remember that there are over 190 member countries in the United Nations. And there are at least 50 other bodies like colonies, territories and **protectorates**. You can choose to study any of them, as long as you think you can find enough information on them.

Studying international organisations

There are thousands of international organisations. Some are well known like the United Nations and the Asian Development Bank. Some are religious organisations that try to help people around the world. There are Christian, Islamic, Jewish and other international religious groups. There are many other non-government international organisations like the World Wildlife Fund, Green Peace and Save the Children. These groups have special interests. You may be able to find representatives from some of these groups in Papua New Guinea. They may be able to help you with information for a project.

Remember that most international organisations are **advocates**. To advocate something means to stand for it or work for it. An advocate wants a result for a cause. An organisation can be an advocate for peace or free trade. Some groups may be an advocate for a religion or a belief.

All advocates will have some bias. If you choose an international organisation, find out what it advocates. What does the organisation want? Is there a bias? How much of a bias is there? What is the other side's view?

For you to try

- What do you know about the following international organisations? What do they want? What do they advocate?
- Can you name any other international organisations?

Greenpeace.

World Wildlife Fund.

The Salvation Army.

Comparative studies

One type of integrating project is to compare Papua New Guinea with other nations. This is called a comparative study. You do it using the social science process. Make sure you choose an area that interests you. You could take one or two topics from the first three chapters. For example:

- Parts of the environment – fresh water, land or vegetation. How are they being protected? How do governments change the way the environment is used or protected? How do cultures change the way the environment is used or protected?
- Natural resources – how are they being used? Are they more valuable in one country than in another? Do governments use them differently?
- Governments – how are the people treated by their government? What type of voting systems and representation do they have? How good are the systems?
- International trade – how is it being developed? How important is it to the nation? Is it important to the government? Are there any special cultural traditions or ideas attached to trade items? How are agricultural trade items grown? Compare agricultural products in Papua New Guinea with another country.
- Culture – compare different festivals, rural settlements, cities, art, songs or dance.
- You could compare the history of Papua New Guinea with another country. You could compare the recent history (20 years) or a longer period (100 years). You could compare the history of settlement in Papua New Guinea and Australia for the last 200 years. You could compare religion in Papua New Guinea with another nation. Are there cultural differences between the same religion in different countries? Does religion change from one country to another?

Remember that in any of these studies you should look for and compare:

- values
- attitudes
- bias
- prejudice
- roles
- adaptation
- innovation.

For example, you could collect pictures of people from different countries. Look what the people are wearing. Use this for a study of culture or some types of trade. Some of the questions you would be asking include:

- What values do the different types of clothing show?
- What roles do the different types of clothing show?
- How is the clothing different or the same in different countries?
- What clothing is an adaptation?
- Is it a cultural adaptation or an environmental adaptation?
- What type of environment or culture is the clothing adapted to?
- Is some of the clothing better than other clothing?
- Is that an attitude or value that you have?
- Is it a bias or prejudice that you have?
- Do you have enough pictures and information?
- Is anything missing?

You could do the same type of study for buildings, transport systems, agricultural systems or other things that you can find pictures of. This is one way to compare different countries with Papua New Guinea. In any of these studies, remember to find something you like. Find something that interests you and become a good social science detective. Find all the information that you can for your project.

International organisations

Another type of integrating project is to study the work and problems of an international organisation. Look at the problems in other countries and Papua New Guinea. Which international organisations try to help with these problems? What they are doing in other countries and in Papua New Guinea? Here are some examples.

What is happening to forests around the world?

Start your observations with reading and talking to people. You discover that South America lost around 4.3 million hectares of forest every year between 2000 and 2005. You find that Oceania lost about 356 000 hectares each year between 2000 and 2005. You know that some of this loss was in Papua New Guinea. You find that North and Central America lost 333 000 hectares of forest each year in the same period. You find that Asia was losing 800 000 hectares each year in the 1990s.

Then you learn that from 2000 to 2005, Asia started gaining one million hectares each year. This seems strange because you know that forests in Indonesia were being destroyed during this time. But then you learn that China has a huge reforestation program. You find that Europe is also increasing forest area, but not as fast as China.

You decide to do a study on an international organisation that helps with forests. Who is helping to protect forests? You start by drawing a map of the world and put in arrows with the information you have found. You could also make a table or a chart with information in it. (Look at examples in this book.)

You discover that the United Nations Development Fund and the United Nations Food and Agriculture Organisation help with forestry projects. You find that there are many non-government agencies that are interested in forests.

You choose one of these organisations and find more information about what it is doing. You talk to a representative of the organisation. You learn that primary forests cover about one third of all forest area. Primary forests show no signs of human activities. You learn that they are being lost or modified at a rate of six million hectares a year. Either they are being completely cleared or changed through selective logging. You find that more forests and trees are being planted. But all this accounts for less than five per cent of world forest areas.

You discover that forests have many purposes. They protect many different types of plants and animals. Some of these can be used for medicines. But they are being destroyed before anyone can study them. Forests protect soil and maintain watersheds. Forests provide many commercial products. They are also important for tourism and recreation.

You draw a picture of what forests can provide. You put the international organisation in this picture. You show what the international organisation is doing.

You learn that with global warming, forests are now even more important to keep carbon out of the atmosphere. Burning forests increases global warming. Planting and conserving forests slows global warming. You draw a diagram or picture to show this.

You study information about the international organisation you have chosen. You read that the World Bank has given money to reforest China. You read that many of the trees planted in China are not watered. Many of them die.

A forest in China.

You go back to the first information you found. You read it again and see that China reported planting millions of hectares of forest. You study more and begin to think that many of the trees have died. You realise that the first article was biased. It hid the truth from you. You realise that more forest is being lost. Some forest is replanted and dies. So dead forest is being counted as forest! You realise this is wrong. But you had to read more and read carefully to find the truth.

You write about the information that you have found. You write about what the organisation is doing in Papua New Guinea and in other places. You finish your report. You wait for two days. You reread your report. Now you can make good conclusions. Now you can write your final conclusions. Your conclusions give your best answers to questions like these:

- What is happening to the world's forests?
- Why is this important?
- What is this international organisation doing about problems with world forests?
- What values, attitudes, biases and prejudices have you discovered in your study?
- What could Papua New Guinea do to help the situation?
- What can individual citizens do?

World forests are just one example of the problems that different international organisations work on. There are many other areas to follow for an integrating study. For example:

- world poverty
- international trade
- international transportation
- migration
- refugees
- loss of natural habitat
- environmental diversity around the world
- diseases like bird flu, malaria, HIV/AIDS, or tuberculosis
- international population growth.

How are world communications changing?

Mobile telephones interest you. You learn that mobile phones are causing cultural, economic and environmental changes. You discover that in 2005 there were more than one billion telephones with fixed lines. And you find that in 2005, there were more than two billion mobile phones.

First you try to find out how many fixed line and mobile phones there are now. Then you can compare them in different countries. Or you could see what international organisations are part of telephone communications. Again, you need to think, 'What interests me? What do I want to find out?'

What is happening with global warming?

How will global warming change the world? You might want to study what has happened with the Kyoto Protocols. You might want to study the problems of rising sea levels. What countries will be affected by this? You might want to study the ocean becoming more acidic. How will this affect fisheries and coral reefs?

Global warming has many advocates and you will need to look carefully at their work. Almost all scientists believe in global warming. But there are advocates against global warming too. Some big oil and coal companies give money to advocates against global warming. They put articles questioning global warming in newspapers and on the radio. You will have to look and listen carefully to find the truth. You will have to watch for bias and prejudice.

One reason for global warming is that we use energy sources that produce carbon. This is related to growing populations and growing economies. Environment, population and economies are all related. Global warming is a large integrated problem. Your study could only cover a small part of this issue.

What is happening with international trade?

You might study whether **competition** or **regulation** is best for a nation. Should countries be part of free trade zones or keep national protection for their products? You might look at economic growth and what must be sacrificed for economic growth. Who benefits from economic growth?

The World Trade Organisation is an international body that promotes international trade. It has faced problems with some countries wanting protection and others wanting free trade. You can find articles about it in the newspaper.

The Melanesian Spearhead Group (MSG) promotes free trade between four member countries. These countries are Papua New Guinea, Vanuatu, Solomon Islands and Fiji. The objectives of the MSG are:

- to promote the free flow of goods and services
- to ensure fair competition
- to expand and develop world trade in the region.

You could find out more about the Melanesian Spearhead Group. What is it doing now?

Fisheries and international trade

THAI CANNED TUNA UNDERCUTS SOLOMONS PRODUCT

WELLINGTON, New Zealand – Solomon Islands Foreign Minister Patteson Oti has expressed concern that a Thai company, which cans tuna it imports from his country, is undercutting the locally manufactured product. He says it is worrying that the Thai company imports frozen tuna from Solomon Islands, cans it and then exports canned tuna back to Solomon Islands. Mr Oti says fishing companies that export frozen tuna to Thailand should revisit whatever arrangements they have with the Thai company because they are hurting Soltai Fishing & Fishing Processing Limited, a company owned by the Western Provincial government and central government. He was speaking at the launch of the Melanesian regional trade and business directory for 2007 in Honiara.

(Radio New Zealand International, April 1)

Many news reports have items about international trade. Here is a radio report about the Solomon Islands. If you are interested in fisheries, it is a type of information you could follow up. You might ask:

- Is this article about trade? Is it about free trade?
- Where is Thailand?
- What is the Thai company doing? Who does that help?
- Does cheap tuna help hungry people in the Solomon Islands? Or is it hurting the Solomon Islands economy?
- Should the Solomon Islands people be canning tuna? What about fresh fish?

You see that there are many values and attitudes to explore in just one news report. You could look at the environmental problems of tuna fishing. You could look at the economic problems of tuna canneries. You could look at the cultural differences between fresh fish and canned fish. You could look at the trade policies of the governments of Thailand and the Solomon Islands.

Why is war and conflict happening?

You may want to see what international agencies are involved in war and conflicts. The United Nations and the Red Cross are two international agencies that are often involved in trying to stop conflicts. There are conflicts over resources and religion. Oil has led to conflict in the Middle East. Religion is part of conflicts in the Middle East, Africa and other parts of Asia.

You might want to look at conflict over resources. There are conflicts that may be caused by global warming. Some experts think that there will be many conflicts over water in the 21st century. This is your century – do you think this will be true?

Kazakhstan, Kyrgyzstan, Tajikistan, Turkmenistan and Uzbekistan have water problems. This is because the Aral Sea is dying. Why is that? And why are all these countries interested in it? Turkmenistan and Uzbekistan have said that they will handle their water problem just between themselves. These two countries have said that the water problem is the 'most pressing topic of current time.' Why don't they want to deal with Kazakhstan, Kyrgyzstan, and Tajikistan at the same time? Just finding out a little information about these countries would be a major project.

How can we have international peace?

There are many organisations that work for international peace. The United Nations, the Melanesian Spearhead Organisation, ecumenical organisations that bring different churches together, and other organisations work for peace. You might study one of these organisations.

Conclusion

The whole world is yours to study. Whatever you study, give yourself time. Be sure the topic is one that you like and one that you are interested in. Check your values and attitudes. Do your best to avoid bias and prejudice.

Remember, there are always at least two sides to any problem. And there are two sides to any study. Be sure you study both sides. Always listen to both sides. That is the most important skill of a good investigator. Give yourself time and you will be a good social science detective.

Glossary

abolished stopped, made illegal

advocates people or organisations that work for a particular cause

arable land that is used for farming

arms military weapons

atheism a belief that there is no god

atmosphere the gases that surround the Earth, including air

atolls coral islands

bias an opinion that comes from a particular direction or viewpoint

candidate a person who stands for election

caste a social class system based on birth

circulation movement; the general circulation of the atmosphere is movement of winds around the Earth

competition to compete for rewards; for example, businesses compete against each other for profits.

continental drift the movement of the continents through plate tectonics

continental shelf the part of the continent that is under water where it meets the sea, sloping down to the deep ocean

corrupt dishonest

currents a large flow of water moving in a particular direction

deciduous trees that lose their leaves in winter

divine god-given, sacred

duties an extra cost placed on imported trade goods (similar to tax)

dynasties ruling families

eligible suitable, with the right qualifications

environment all of the physical things (whether natural or made by people) in a particular place

evaporates when water heats up and turns into water vapour

evergreen trees that keep their leaves all year round

extinction when a particular species dies out

finite limited

fundamentalist extremely conservative

globalisation the spread of culture, products and systems around the world; also a world economic system based on free trade

global warming the heating up of the Earth's atmosphere

globe a round shape; the Earth is often described as a globe

greenhouse gases the gases that create global warming; carbon dioxide, methane and water vapour

grid a series of lines that run parallel and perpendicular to each other

hemispheres the two halves of the planet Earth; the Northern Hemisphere is above the Equator and the Southern Hemisphere is below it

hereditary handed down through a family

hieroglyphics a set of symbols used as an early form of writing

humanity all the people on Earth

hypothesis an idea or question upon which research can be based

icons images or symbols of a culture

indentured servants people who sell themselves into service for a fixed period of time

infinite never-ending

irrigation systems made by humans to bring water to food crops and animals often using trenches and canals

latitude the location of a place north or south of the Equator

longitude the location of a place east or west of the Prime Meridian

magma molten rock

mariners sailors

market economy an economic system driven by supply and demand in free markets

minority a small group, less than half

monarchs leaders who are born into their position

mummies preserved human bodies after death (some animals too)

non-renewable finite or limited

orbits moves around in a circular path

patron sponsor or supporter

population density the number of people living in a certain area, such as a square kilometre

prehistory the period before recorded history

precipitation rain, hail, sleet and snow

predictions ideas about what will happen in the future

preferences preferred choices

prejudice an opinion formed without any reason or experience

Prime Meridian a navigation line that runs from North to South Poles, through Greenwich, England

protectorates small colonies or territories

racism the belief that people are different depending on the colour of their skin or the country they belong to

raw materials the basic goods used to create something; oil is a raw material that is used to make fuel

regulation regulations are rules or laws made by a government

rotates spins around in a circle on an axis

sects small religious groups

sphere a circular shape, like a globe

status position in society

stereotypes a biased view of a person from a particular place or culture

stratosphere the outer layer of the atmosphere

submerged underwater

subsidies payments given by the government to help businesses (often given to farmers in Europe and the United States of America)

surplus extra

taxes money paid to the government by citizens

tectonic plates the structures beneath the continents and oceans

universe all of space to include our world, the sun, stars and beyond; also called the cosmos

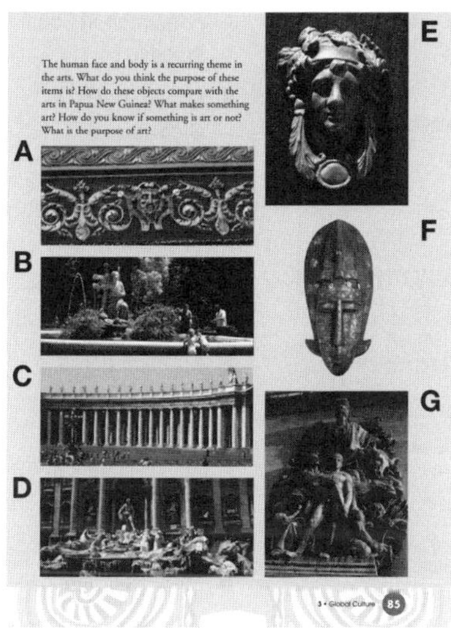

The human face and body is a recurring theme in the arts. What do you think the purpose of these items is? How do these objects compare with the arts in Papua New Guinea? What makes something art? How do you know if something is art or not? What is the purpose of art?

3 • Global Culture 85

- **A** Latin American wall ornamentation
- **B** Fountain in Europe
- **C** The Vatican in Rome, Italy
- **D** The Trevi Fountain in Rome, Italy
- **E** Latin American door ornament
- **F** African mask
- **G** Statue in Europe

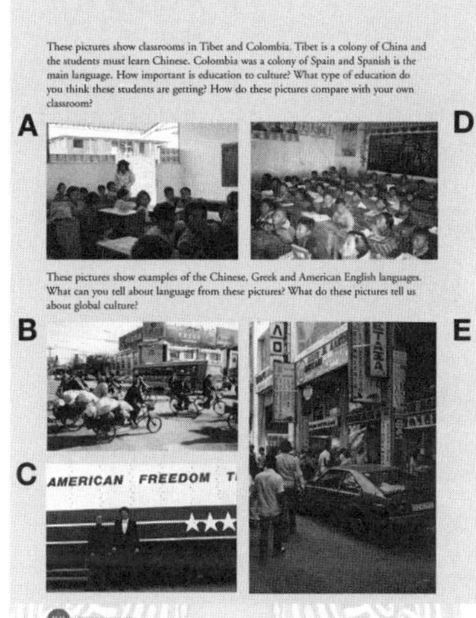

These pictures show classrooms in Tibet and Colombia. Tibet is a colony of China and the students must learn Chinese. Colombia was a colony of Spain and Spanish is the main language. How important is education to culture? What type of education do you think these students are getting? How do these pictures compare with your own classroom?

These pictures show examples of the Chinese, Greek and American English languages. What can you tell about language from these pictures? What do these pictures tell us about global culture?

88 Social Science Grade 8

- **A** Classroom in Colombia
- **B** China
- **C** America
- **D** Classroom in Tibet
- **E** Greece

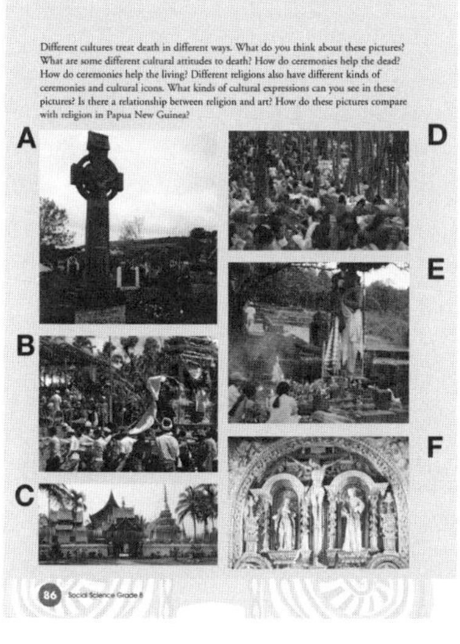

Different cultures treat death in different ways. What do you think about these pictures? What are some different cultural attitudes to death? How do ceremonies help the dead? How do ceremonies help the living? Different religions also have different kinds of ceremonies and cultural icons. What kinds of cultural expressions can you see in these pictures? Is there a relationship between religion and art? How do these pictures compare with religion in Papua New Guinea?

86 Social Science Grade 8

- **A** Graveyard in Ireland
- **B** Funeral procession in Bali
- **C** Temples in Thailand
- **D** Buddhist ceremony in Burma (Myanmar)
- **E** Prayer ceremony in Laos
- **F** Catholic church in Ecuador

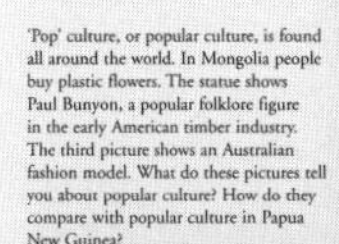

'Pop' culture, or popular culture, is found all around the world. In Mongolia people buy plastic flowers. The statue shows Paul Bunyon, a popular folklore figure in the early American timber industry. The third picture shows an Australian fashion model. What do these pictures tell you about popular culture? How do they compare with popular culture in Papua New Guinea?

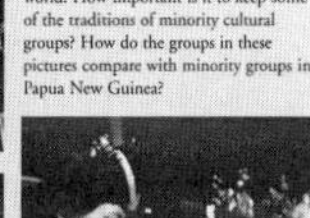

Sub-cultures, or minority groups, contribute to larger cultures around the world. How important is it to keep some of the traditions of minority cultural groups? How do the groups in these pictures compare with minority groups in Papua New Guinea?

3 • Global Culture 89

- **A** Australian fashion model
- **B** Pacific Islanders
- **C** Minority ethnic group from southern China
- **D** Statue of Paul Bunyan
- **E** Flower stall in Mongolia
- **F** Minority ethnic group from southern China

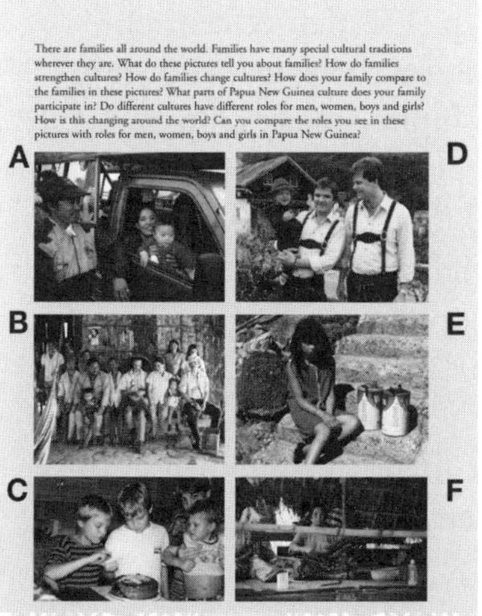

There are families all around the world. Families have many special cultural traditions wherever they are. What do these pictures tell you about families? How do families strengthen cultures? How do families change cultures? How does your family compare to the families in these pictures? What parts of Papua New Guinea culture does your family participate in? Do different cultures have different roles for men, women, boys and girls? How is this changing around the world? Can you compare the roles you see in these pictures with roles for men, women, boys and girls in Papua New Guinea?

3 • Global Culture 87

- **A** Family in Laos
- **B** South American family
- **C** American boys
- **D** Austrian men in traditional dress
- **E** Latin American girl carrying kerosene
- **F** Female weaver in Thailand

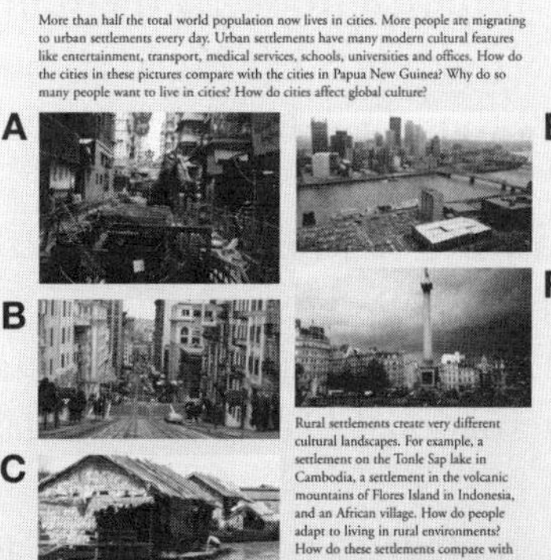

More than half the total world population now lives in cities. More people are migrating to urban settlements every day. Urban settlements have many modern cultural features like entertainment, transport, medical services, schools, universities and offices. How do the cities in these pictures compare with the cities in Papua New Guinea? Why do so many people want to live in cities? How do cities affect global culture?

Rural settlements create very different cultural landscapes. For example, a settlement on the Tonle Sap lake in Cambodia, a settlement in the volcanic mountains of Flores Island in Indonesia, and an African village. How do people adapt to living in rural environments? How do these settlements compare with rural areas in Papua New Guinea?

90 Social Science Grade 8

- **A** Hong Kong
- **B** San Francisco, United States of America
- **C** Tonle Sap, Cambodia
- **D** Village in Africa
- **E** Baltimore, United States of America
- **F** London, England
- **G** Flores Island, Indonesia

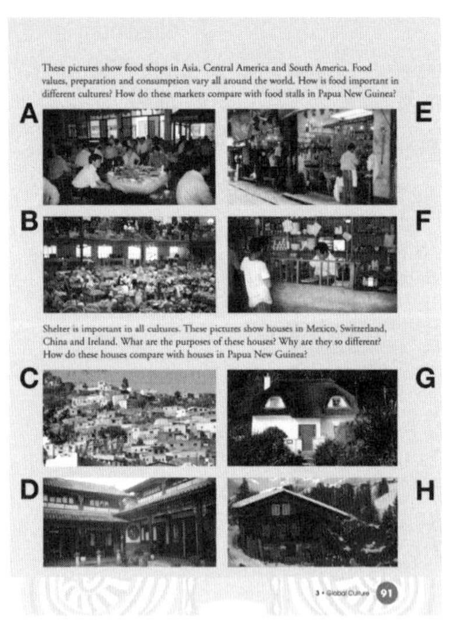

These pictures show food shops in Asia, Central America and South America. Food values, preparation and consumption vary all around the world. How is food important in different cultures? How do these markets compare with food stalls in Papua New Guinea?

A E B F

Shelter is important in all cultures. These pictures show houses in Mexico, Switzerland, China and Ireland. What are the purposes of these houses? Why are they so different? How do these houses compare with houses in Papua New Guinea?

C G D H

3 • Global Culture 91

- **A** Food stall in Asia
- **B** Market in Central America
- **C** Houses in Mexico
- **D** Courtyard in China
- **E** Meat market in Asia
- **F** Trade store in South America
- **G** Cottage in Ireland
- **H** House in Switzerland

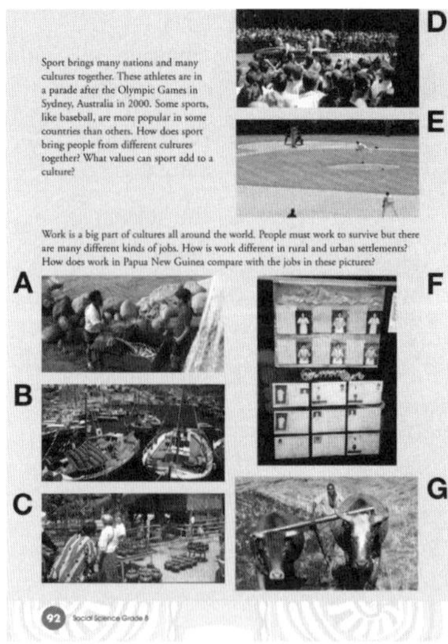

Sport brings many nations and many cultures together. These athletes are in a parade after the Olympic Games in Sydney, Australia in 2000. Some sports, like baseball, are more popular in some countries than others. How does sport bring people from different cultures together? What values can sport add to a culture?

D E

Work is a big part of cultures all around the world. People must work to survive but there are many different kinds of jobs. How is work different in rural and urban settlements? How does work in Papua New Guinea compare with the jobs in these pictures?

A B C F G

92 Social Science Grade 8

- **A** Fishermen in South America
- **B** Fishing boats in Greece
- **C** Village stall selling clay pots in Burma (Myanmar)
- **D** Athletes on parade in Sydney, Australia
- **E** Baseball game in United States of America
- **F** Advertisement for domestic workers in Hong Kong
- **G** Farmers in Africa

Acknowledgments

The author and publisher wish to thank the following copyright holders for granting permission to reproduce their material.

AAP Image, p. 132 (right); Bridgeman Art Library, p. 52 (right); Center for International Earth Science Information Network world population density map, p. 28; Corbis, pp. 29 (bottom), 48; Fotolia, pp. 17 (top), 18 (top), 25 (bottom), 46; Getty Images, p. 132 (left & centre); Istockphoto, pp. 18 (bottom), 19, 27, 31, 35, 42, 57, 59 (right), 62, 69 (bottom), 100 (top), 109, 110 (top), 112 (bottom), 114 (top), 115 (bottom), 116, 135; Jupiter Images, pp. 3, 12, 17 (bottom), 25 (top), 39, 43, 47, 56, 58, 59 (left), 85 (right centre), 110 (bottom), 111 (top), 112 (top), 113 (bottom), 114 (bottom), 115 (top); Photolibrary, pp. 30 (bottom), 100 (bottom); Photolibrary/Alamy, pp. 49, 52 (left), 73, 75, 89 (top left); Ashley Spicer, pp. 16, 69 (top); Stockxchange, p. 120; UN Population and Vital Statistics Report population chart, p. 27; US Census Bureau International Data Base population growth chart, p. 26

Every effort has been made to trace the original source of copyright material contained in this book. The publisher would be pleased to hear from copyright holders to rectify any errors or omissions.

A Timeline of Important World Events

The table shows a few of the many notable human events over the centuries. Students could make their own timelines as a project and explain why they think the events they choose are important. Other project ideas are given in the timeline.

Note: BP means the number of years 'Before Present'. The birth of Christ is year 1 and it starts the first century of our calendar. Year 1 to year 100 is the 1st century. We are now in the 21st century.

Another way of recording dates is to use AD and BC. AD is Latin for Anno Domini (the Year of our Lord) and BC stands for 'Before Christ'. We use the more recent convention of BP in the timeline. You can update the timeline by adding a year for each year after 2008.

How many years ago?	What happened?	Approximate date
600 000 mid-point estimate	Evidence of Peking Man, a type of early human in China. (Evidence of early humans in China goes back at least 1.6 million years, and in Africa for up to 4 million years.)	700000 to 500000 BP
200 000	Evidence of modern humans in Africa.	200000 BP
70 000	Evidence of successful migration by modern humans out of Africa. Recent evidence indicates that these modern humans may have mixed with older human types already in Asia.	70000 BP
40 000 – 10 000	Independent invention of forest management and agriculture in New Guinea.	40000 – 10000 BP
12 000	Humans start to take advantage of climatic warming and the end of the last ice age to develop complex agriculture and settlements.	12000 BP
5 000	Sumerians in the Middle East develop a number system (with a base of 60) that we still use for time and degrees in a sphere (latitude and longitude).	5000 BP
4 700	Corn is domesticated in America and becomes the base for civilisations in North, South and Central America, before Europeans and African slaves arrive some 4 200 years later.	4700 BP
2 571	Birth of Siddartha Gautama who becomes the Buddha and founds the Buddhist religion.	2571 BP
2 508	Earliest complete commentary that is still in existence on Vedic (Hindu) religious beliefs. It is called the *Nirukta*. It lists three great gods: Fire, Storm or Wind, and Sun.	2508 BP

How many years ago?	What happened?	Approximate date
2 476 mid-point	The life of Plato, one of the three most important classical Greek philosophers. (The other two are Socrates – his teacher – and Aristotle, who studied his works about 50 years after Plato had died).	2436–2356 BP
2 335	Alexander the Great (a Greek leader) starts to invade India. This is the high point for spreading Greek ideas by force. Long after Alexander's empire is gone, the ideas will continue to influence thinking in many parts of the world. (A project could look at these ideas continuing today.)	2335 BP
2 300	Euclid, a Greek mathematician invents the principles for geometry that are used for the next 2 000 years.	2300 BP
1 975	Pontius Pilate, Governor of Judea for the Roman Empire, condemns Jesus Christ to death by crucifixion.	33
1 695	The Roman Emperor grants the right to freedom of religion to all inhabitants of the Roman Empire. Eighty years later Christianity is made the official religion of Rome, and other sects are forbidden.	313
1 619 mid-point	Life of St Augustine, the Bishop of Hippo in North Africa and the most important Christian philosopher of the first 1000 years of Christianity. He worked to combine classical Greek philosophy with Christian theology.	354–430
758 mid-point	The life of St Thomas Aquinas, the most famous European philosopher and theologian of the middle ages. He combined Christian thinking with earlier classic Greek ideas.	1226–1274
698	Bubonic plague starts in China and spreads to Europe by 1347. By the middle of 1300 it had killed almost a third of all Europeans. (A project could discuss the effects of one in three people dying today.)	1310
553	Guttenberg publishes the Bible and starts the period of the printing press. Knowledge can be spread widely. Latin is used as the 'lingua franca' for scientific communication in Europe. (A project could look at changes in language and how much later Tok Pisin will be used as the 'lingua franca' for Papua New Guinea.)	1455

How many years ago?	What happened?	Approximate date
523 mid-point	The life of Leonardo da Vinci, a famous Italian artist, inventor and scientific experimenter. He lived in Europe during the time of the Renaissance (meaning 'rebirth'). Many modern ideas started in this period. (A project could explore new ideas from the Renaissance.)	1452–1519
519	Christopher Columbus starts European exploration of the Americas, which led to the establishment of the Spanish American empire, Portuguese Brazil, and other European colonies.	1492
466	Copernicus, a European mathematician, publishes a work that demonstrates that the Earth orbits the Sun. (He may have known this for decades but feared to contradict the faith at that time, which declared that Earth was the centre of the universe.)	1543
413 mid-point	The life of Sir Francis Bacon, who promoted scientific or empirical thought.	1561–1629
419 mid-point	The life of William Shakespeare, considered to be the greatest writer in the English Language.	1564–1616
340 mid-point	The life of John Locke, a British philosopher who made important contributions to ideas about civil liberty and religious tolerance in Great Britain.	1632–1704
365	Qing Dynasty rules China for 268 years. It was followed by a weak republic for another 48 years.	1644 1911
222	John Fitch successfully launches a steamboat on the Delaware River in North America.	1786
219	The United States of America holds the first election after winning the war of Independence with Great Britain.	1789
216	The monarchy is abolished in France in a violent and bloody revolution, after years of royals mistreating many French citizens.	1792
188	The woman's 'suffrage' movement began, seeking the right for women to vote in many countries around the world. New Zealand was the first country to allow women to vote in 1893. Some countries in the Middle East still do not allow women to vote today.	1820s

How many years ago?	What happened?	Approximate date
143	Francis Field lays the first transatlantic cable for telegraph communications between the United States of America and Europe. The telephone was invented in 1876. The communication revolution gained speed and has not stopped to this day.	1866
163 mid-point	Life of Charles Darwin, co-founder of the theory of evolution.	1809–1882
111 mid-point	Life of Sigmund Freud, an Austrian scientist who invented the theory of psychoanalysis and explored the power of sex to influence human behaviour.	1856–1939
107	Australia's five colonies join to become the Commonwealth of Australia.	1901
105	The Wright brothers achieve mechanised flight.	1903
89	The Treaty of Versailles ends World War I. The treaty punishes Germany with very high fines. Many say this action leads to World War II.	1919
67 mid-point	World War II kills some 40 million people. It ends with development planning instead of punishment for the losers, resulting in the European Union.	1939–1945
59	Establishment of Communist rule in China. The People's Republic of China is founded.	1949
33	Independence is granted to Papua New Guinea.	1975
18	Boris Yeltsin takes over as the first President of Russia. The USSR has collapsed and the communist system that started in 1919 ends.	1991
12	The first cloned sheep is born and named Dolly.	1996
1	The United Nations Secretary General warns the world that international co-operation and action is vital to prevent a global warming catastrophe.	2007